Perceptions of the Crusades from the Nineteenth to the Twenty-First Century

Engaging the Crusades is a series of volumes which offer windows into a newly emerging field of historical study: the memory and legacy of the crusades. Together these volumes examine the reasons behind the enduring resonance of the crusades and present the memory of crusading in the modern period as a productive, exciting and much needed area of investigation.

Perceptions of the Crusades from the Nineteenth to the Twenty-First Century explores the ways in which the crusades have been used in the last two centuries, including the varying deployment of crusading rhetoric and imagery in both the East and the West. It considers the scope and impact of crusading memory from the nineteenth and into the twentieth century, engaging with nineteenth-century British lending libraries, literary uses of crusading tales, wartime postcard propaganda, memories of Saladin and crusades in the Near East and the works of modern crusade historians.

Demonstrating the breadth of material encompassed by this subject and offering methodological suggestions for continuing its progress, *Perceptions of the Crusades from the Nineteenth to the Twenty-First Century* is essential reading for modern historians, military historians and historians of memory and medievalism.

Mike Horswell recently completed his PhD at Royal Holloway, University of London, where he is a Visiting Lecturer. His book – *The Rise and Fall of British Crusader Medievalism, c.1825–1945* – was published in early 2018; he is currently researching and writing about the memory and use of the crusades in the modern era.

Jonathan Phillips is Professor of the History of the Crusades at Royal Holloway, University of London. He has published extensively on the history of the medieval crusades, including works on the Second and Fourth Crusades, and is the editor of the forthcoming *Cambridge History of the Crusades.* His next book, to be published in 2019, is on the life and legacy of Saladin.

ENGAGING THE CRUSADES

THE MEMORY AND LEGACY OF THE CRUSADES

SERIES EDITORS
JONATHAN PHILLIPS AND MIKE HORSWELL

Engaging the Crusades
The Memory and Legacy of Crusading
Series Editors: Jonathan Phillips and Mike Horswell, Royal Holloway,
University of London, UK.

Engaging the Crusades is a series of volumes which offer initial windows into the ways in which the crusades have been used in the last two centuries; demonstrating that the memory of the crusades is an important and emerging subject. Together these studies suggest that the memory of the crusades, in the modern period, is a productive, exciting and much needed area of investigation.

In this series:

Perceptions of the Crusades from the Nineteenth to the Twenty-First Century
Engaging the Crusades, Volume One
Edited by Mike Horswell and Jonathan Phillips

For more information about this series, please visit: https://www.routledge.com/Engaging-the-Crusades/book-series/ETC

Perceptions of the Crusades from the Nineteenth to the Twenty-First Century

Engaging the Crusades, Volume One

**Edited by Mike Horswell
and Jonathan Phillips**

LONDON AND NEW YORK

First published 2018
by Routledge
2 Park Square, Milton Park, Abingdon, Oxon OX14 4RN

and by Routledge
605 Third Avenue, New York, NY 10017

First issued in paperback 2021

Routledge is an imprint of the Taylor & Francis Group, an informa business

British Library Cataloguing-in-Publication Data
A catalogue record for this book is available from the British Library

Library of Congress Cataloging-in-Publication Data
A catalog record for this book has been requested

ISBN 13: 978-1-03-209534-9 (pbk)
ISBN 13: 978-1-138-06601-4 (hbk)

Typeset in Times New Roman
by codeMantra

Contents

Figures

x   *Figures*

Acknowledgements

This book represents the first product of the stimulating conversations begun in London in September 2015 at the conference *Engaging the Crusades: Reflected, Refracted, Invented*, and flourishing since. Accordingly, our debts are broad: our thanks are due to all participants in that conference whose labour will be reflected in subsequent volumes in this series, and to the supporters of that event – the History Department at Royal Holloway, University of London, the Society for the Study of the Crusades and the Latin East and the Institute for Historical Research. Thanks also to participants in this volume, whose patience and grace in engaging with the editorial process has made this possible. And thanks to all at Routledge – not least our editor Laura Pilsworth – for providing the space for this discussion. We particularly wish to thank Adam Knobler for his generous advice. Finally, many thanks to our families for their continuing support of us!

Abbreviations

CUP   Cambridge University Press
FO   Reference for Foreign Office papers, held at TNA, Kew, London
HO   Reference for Home Office papers, held at TNA, Kew, London
MUP   Manchester University Press
ODNB   *Oxford Dictionary of National Biography*
OUP   Oxford University Press
TNA   The National Archives, Kew, London

Frequently used references:

Knobler, 'Holy Wars'   Adam Knobler, 'Holy Wars, Empires, and the Portability of the Past: The Modern Uses of Medieval Crusades', *Comparative Studies in Society and History* 48 (2006), pp. 293–325.

Siberry, *New Crusaders*   Elizabeth Siberry, *The New Crusaders: Images of the Crusades in the 19th and Early 20th Centuries* (Aldershot: Ashgate, 2000).

Contributors

Felix Hinz is Professor of Politics, History and Didactics at the University of Education in Freiburg im Breisgau who has published on the use of the crusades in German, French and English literature – *Mythos Kreuzzüge* (2014). His interests include concepts and reception of 'Holy War' through the ages as well as the processes of historical narration.

Mike Horswell recently completed his PhD at Royal Holloway, University of London, where he is a Visiting Lecturer. His book – *The Rise and Fall of British Crusader Medievalism, c. 1825–1945* – was published in early 2018; he is currently researching and writing about the memory and use of the crusades in the modern era.

Jonathan Phillips is Professor of the History of the Crusades at Royal Holloway, University of London. He has published extensively on the history of the medieval crusades, including works on the Second and Fourth Crusades, and is the editor of the forthcoming *Cambridge History of the Crusades*. His next book, to be published in 2019, is on the life and legacy of Saladin.

Elizabeth Siberry has published many articles and chapters on nineteenth- and twentieth-century images of the crusades in Britain, most notably in her book *The New Crusaders* (2000). Her current research examines how families memorialised the crusades and crusading ancestors through legend, art and architecture.

Kristin Skottki is Junior Professor of Medieval History at the University of Bayreuth. She has mainly published on the medieval and modern historiography of the First Crusade, as in her monograph *Christen, Muslime und der Erste Kreuzzug* (2015). Her current research focuses on late medieval piety and medievalism.

Introduction
Engaging the crusades

Jonathan Phillips and Mike Horswell

Series introduction

The crusades and ideas of crusading have long held a place in our collective imaginations. To a nineteenth-century Frenchman it was part of his heritage; to a twenty-first-century US president, it was an image to conjure in his wish to defeat al-Qaeda. To a nineteenth-century Egyptian facing the Emperor Napoleon, the crusaders had simply come back again after 550 years; to a twentieth-century Egyptian president, Saladin's achievements were a template for action. To a Norwegian right-wing extremist, the Knights Templar offered an example of striving against the forces of Islam; to the propagandists of the so-called Islamic State (IS/ISIL/ISIS), the crusades were another expression of Western religious expansionism which had never ended.[1] Crusading, then, has proven to possess an enduring legacy.

This series of essays aims both to draw together and to give substance to a newly emerging field of historical study: the memory and the legacy of the crusades. The crusades – as illustrated by the breadth of examples above – have remained a potent concept, although their meaning has been contested. This is a topic that stretches back down the centuries and takes many different forms. The question overarching the field is this: how and why has an idea created in the late eleventh century resonated down the ages and, at times, echoed so powerfully?[2] These volumes seek to examine the means by which this happened and to provide illustrations of the many, varied forms in which the memory and the legacy of the crusades have persisted and been employed.

Moreover, perceptions of what constituted the crusades have varied. Over 900 years of history writing on the crusades has seen changing interpretations of what the medieval expeditions were, what motivated the crusaders, what the effects of the crusades were, when they ended and – not least – what counted as crusading. Crusade historiography constitutes an existing field of study in itself, but one which cannot be divorced from broader assessments of how crusading has been variously understood.[3] Thus, considerations of academic perspectives on the crusades find a home here alongside studies which contextualise popular perceptions and draw connections between the two.

At root, this is a matter of cultural memory, and in that sense, all of these studies are indebted, consciously or not, to memory studies. Paul Connerton argued that 'concerning social memory in particular, we may note that images of the past commonly legitimate a present social order.' He notes that 'our experience of the present very largely depends upon our knowledge of the past [...] past factors tend to influence, or distort, our experience of the present'.[4] Collective memory of any given event, French sociologist Maurice Halbwachs proposed, could be heterogeneous across a society as there would be the potential for as many different uses or needs as there were subgroups within that society – it is more accurate therefore to talk of *memories*.[5] '[T]he remembered past,' Geoffrey Cubitt has concluded, 'is in practice, always multiple and contestable, mutable and elusive.'[6] In these ways, memories of the crusades can be understood to be flexible and depend for their meaning on the societies in which they have been embodied. This series sits at the interface between memory, medievalism and crusade studies.[7]

We can explore the subject through an enormous range of evidence. Relevant material is found in literature, educational works, visual sources, academic historiography, drama, music and opera, as well as through political and religious texts, ceremonies and performances. Crusading has been used at popular, mass-culture levels, as well as in carefully framed ideological moments (these are, of course, not mutually exclusive). It can also be employed to inspire, enflame, entertain, educate, misinform and provoke. The studies included, therefore, will address a wide range of events, groups, individuals and contexts, whilst discovering and evaluating perceptions and uses of the crusades.

This project builds on foundations established by (among others) Adam Knobler, Elizabeth Siberry, Emmanuel Sivan and Jonathan Riley-Smith, as well as a plethora of specific works which often address material on the memory of the crusades sidelong.[8] What we have here is a subject that draws together previously disparate studies and gives a broader cultural, historical and geographical context to such work. The *Engaging the Crusades* volumes mark the emergence of an important new subject area. As we have discovered, this is a topic that continues to grow as scholars from across the globe realise their work can feed into this project.[9] Since our conference in September 2015 further areas of interest have emerged: the memory of the crusades in the Spanish conquest of South America, the legacy of the Fourth Crusade and the Sack of Constantinople (1204) in early modern and modern Greece, the image of Saladin in Southeast Asia, family memories of crusading ancestors, the re-inscription of Iraqi textbooks after the Gulf War and representations of crusading in computer games, to name but a few. For all the wrong reasons (the emergence of IS being the most troubling, but also, for example, the presence of individuals dressed as crusaders in alt-right rallies in Europe) the memory and the legacy of the crusades are topical issues to address. What we hope to offer here is a forum to enable scholarly research into this subject to cohere and to blossom.

Volume one: perceptions of the crusades from the nineteenth to the twenty-first century

Some historians regard Napoleon's conquest of the crusading order of the Knights of Saint John on Malta (1798) as an end point for crusading. This is, however, only a marker of convenience. What becomes strikingly apparent from around the same time onwards is a resurgence and revival in the use of crusade ideas in both Western Europe and the Near East. European expansion into the Eastern Mediterranean in the nineteenth and twentieth centuries led to a greater fascination with the lands and history of the crusades alongside material involvement in the form of consular presence, archaeological exploration, tourism, pilgrimage, heritage preservation and direct control.[10] As European power and influence in the Mediterranean increased, Britain, France, Germany, Belgium, Russia and Spain, for example, all harked back to a crusading past. As the Crimean War demonstrated, all antagonists flexed ideological muscles in the context of imperial competition and vying for power and drew on crusading rhetoric.[11] This came during the development and emergence of the distinct, professional disciplines of history and archaeology, which fed off and fuelled this increased contact.

Crusading proved extremely flexible in accommodating the requirements of the nation-builders of Europe, and beyond, whether legitimising particular regimes, serving as a 'golden age' to hark back to or as the background and landscape for the creation of national heroes. Crusading pasts, real or imagined, continued to occupy central places in European national self-imaginings in the nineteenth and early twentieth centuries. Associating modern nations with medieval figures asserted some form of continuity between medieval and modern ages. Moreover, 'The virtues these crusaders represented', Christopher

Tyerman has observed, 'were of generalised national spirit not precise political arrangements. Nonetheless, such reimagining securely incorporated the crusades into national histories and public consciousness.'[12]

From the perspective of the modern Near East, a blend of factors recommended crusading parallelism. First of all, Western aggression and invasions, coupled with loss of life, land and freedom, appeared to be repeating themselves. Secondly, and more importantly, the medieval crusades were defeated. Saladin drew together the Muslim Near East and in 1187 recovered the holy city of Jerusalem for Islam and for the rulers of al Sham; just over 100 years later, the Christians were finally ejected. This was a narrative to inspire – one that could persistently be seen as relevant and topical. To pit West versus East and then to run a sequence from the medieval crusades through to the colonial age, the Mandate era and into Zionism as well, can form a compelling argument to some. Furthermore, during the nineteenth century this was a narrative which the West did much to encourage through its own self-image as treading in the footsteps of their crusading ancestors, something that has not entirely disappeared today. The Western presence in the Mediterranean also generated a whole new series of challenges for the people of the Near East. These concerned, for example, the advent of technology or relationships between community structures. In seeking responses to these questions, some of which included Western-derived influences such as nationalism, people looked to history. In the circumstances, they did not have to look far for a model to rally around: Saladin.[13] The Kurdish hero was adopted (and adapted) by Arab Nationalists in the early twentieth century, by Gamal Nasser in Egypt, Saddam Hussein in Iraq and by both Hafez and Bashar al-Assad in Syria, as well as being more broadly feted in school books and popular culture throughout the last two centuries. More recently, the crusades have been employed as a symbol of continuous Western aggression by both Osama bin Laden and IS.

This volume will provide an initial window into the ways in which the crusades have been used in the last two centuries, taking seriously the popular penumbra of crusading memory and considering its shape, scope and impact from the nineteenth into the twentieth century. The chapters here engage with varying uses of crusading rhetoric and imagery in both East and West, from Sir Walter Scott to modern crusade historians, in order to indicate both the breadth of material the topic can encompass and different methodological approaches. Elizabeth Siberry's pathfinding chapter builds on her previous investigations of crusading memory by considering ways in which it is possible to uncover what the Victorians were reading about the crusades; it represents an important provocation to integrate studies of cultural reception into evaluations of how crusading was understood. Mike Horswell's chapter seeks to bring together examples of juvenile literature written by British author-educators and establish how they were promoting Victorian values through crusading stories. In examining German postcards printed during the First World War, Felix Hinz highlights the German uses of holy war imagery and crusading rhetoric to frame the conflict and imagine the Kaiser. Jonathan Phillips' chapter overturns the assumption – long held by crusade scholars – that the East had forgotten the crusades as he shines a light on the long memory of Saladin and the crusades between 1880 and 1925. Finally, contributing to the ongoing discussions among crusade historians, Kristin Skottki reflects on historiographical traditions and how the perceptions and assumptions of historical practitioners can shade their work.

Crusading, then, has had a special resonance and power. The longevity and diversity of crusading – while maintained at different levels of intensity between the West and the Near East – kept the idea, or the memory of the idea, 'in play'. This series seeks to elucidate how, where and why this has, and continues to, take place.

Notes

1 See Jonathan Phillips, *Holy Warriors* (London, 2010), pp. 312–55.
2 Posed by Adam Knobler in his 2006 article as 'The trans-national ubiquity of crusading images is striking. How and why did an 850-year-old series of conflicts become such an effective language in communicating ideas between classes and societies?'; Knobler, 'Holy Wars', p. 294.
3 Norman Housley, *Contesting the Crusades* (Oxford, 2006); Christopher Tyerman, *The Debate on the Crusades* (Manchester, 2011).
4 Paul Connerton, *How Societies Remember* (Cambridge, 1989), p. 3.
5 Lewis A. Coser, 'Introduction: Maurice Halbwachs 1877–1945', in Maurice Halbwachs, *On Collective Memory*, ed. and trans. Lewis A. Coser (London, 1992), p. 22.
6 Geoffrey Cubitt, *History and Memory* (Manchester, 2007), p. 242.
7 For the emerging application of ideas of memory and medievalism studies to the crusades, Mike Horswell has proposed the phrase 'crusader medievalism'; Mike Horswell, *The Rise and Fall of British Crusader Medievalism, c. 1825–1945* (Abingdon, 2018). See also Kristin Skottki's chapter in this volume.
8 Knobler, 'Holy Wars'. Most notably for Siberry: Elizabeth Siberry, 'Images of the Crusades in the Nineteenth and Twentieth Centuries', in *The Oxford Illustrated History of the Crusades* Siberry, *New Crusaders*; Emmanuel Sivan, *L'Islam et la Croisade* (Paris, 1968); and Emmanuel Sivan, 'Modern Arabic Historiography', *Asian and African Studies* 8 (1972), pp. 104–49. For Jonathan Riley-Smith, see Jonathan Riley-Smith, 'Revival and Survival', in *Oxford Illustrated History of the Crusades*, ed.

Riley-Smith, pp. 386–91; Jonathan Riley-Smith, *The Crusades, Christianity, and Islam* (Chichester, 2008).

9 For example, see Felix Hinz, *Kreuzzüge des Mittelalters und der Neuzeit* (Hildesheim, 2015); Joseph Shadur, *Young Travelers to Jerusalem: The Holy Land in American and English Juvenile Literature, 1785–1940* (Ramat Gan, 1999); Matthias Determann, 'The Crusades in Arab School Textbooks', *Islam and Christian-Muslim Relations* 19 (2008), pp. 199–214; Ines Anna Guhe, 'Crusade Narratives in French and German History Textbooks, 1871–1914', *European Review of History: Revue Europeenne D'histoire* 20 (2013), pp. 367–82; Nickolas Haydock and Edward L. Risden, eds., *Hollywood in the Holy Land: Essays on Film Depictions of the Crusades and Christian-Muslim Clashes* (London, 2008); Eitan Bar-Yosef, 'The Last Crusade? British Propaganda and the Palestine Campaign, 1917–18', *Journal of Contemporary History* 36 (2001), pp. 87–109; Stefan Goebel, 'Britain's "Last Crusade": From War Propaganda to War Commemoration, c.1914–1930', in *Justifying War: Propaganda, Politics and the Modern Age*, eds. David Welch and Jo Fox (Basingstoke, 2012), pp. 159–76; Albert Marrin, *The Last Crusade: The Church of England in the First World War* (Durham, NC, 1974).

10 See Astrid Swenson, 'Crusader Heritages and Imperial Preservation', *Past and Present* 226 (2015), pp. 27–56.

11 For example, Kim Munholland, 'Michaud's History of the Crusades and the French Crusade in Algeria under Louis-Philippe', in *The Popularization of Images: Visual Culture under the July Monarchy*, eds. Petra ten-Doesschate Chu and Gabriel P. Weisberg (Princeton, NJ, 1994), pp. 144–65; Adam Knobler, 'Holy Wars'. For the Crimean War, see Orlando Figes, *Crimea: The Last Crusade* (London, 2011).

12 Tyerman, *Debate*, p. 115.

13 Jonathan Phillips, *Saladin* (London, 2019).

1   The crusades
Nineteenth-century readers' perspectives

Elizabeth Siberry

Whilst the existence of a book does not necessarily mean that it was read or indeed influenced contemporary perceptions of the crusading movement, there are some sources that provide an indication of what was read and by whom in Britain during the nineteenth century, and these provide a glimpse of the variety of attitudes towards the crusades in this period and what shaped them. This is important in piecing together a jigsaw of how the crusades were seen and described at this time and the influence of particular works and perspectives.

A number of printed catalogues of major public and private libraries during this period have survived, and research has shown the wide range of other ways in which readers could access books, from coffee houses to booksellers, schools and universities, clubs and book groups.[1] Different libraries served different readers. There were public (free) libraries, subscription or circulating libraries and private libraries in many of the great houses, and private in this context did not necessarily mean for the exclusive use of the owners. Indeed by 1850, 'any person could borrow any kind of literature and read it in his (or indeed her) own domestic space, or use an institutional library and socialise with like-minded people'.[2]

The records of the London Library in St James' Square, London, provide a good starting point. A private subscription library founded in 1841 and still operating today, it included many prominent figures amongst its members. The prime mover behind its establishment was the historian and writer Thomas Carlyle, who summarised its aim as 'A collection of standard books in various languages, calculated for the use of literary men and of all who prosecute self-instruction and rational entertainment by reading.' Carlyle noted that there were public libraries in other towns in England and in major cities throughout Europe, but in London, there was no lending library capable of 'supplying the intellectual wants of its inhabitants'. Carlyle even used language derived from the crusades to describe his project. In an essay, 'Signs of the times', he wrote of Peter the Hermit 'rugged steel-clad Europe trembled beneath his words and followed him whither he listed' and referred to himself as another Peter leading 'the crusade for the foundation of the London Library'.[3]

By the beginning of 1841 the Library had some five hundred subscribers, including Charles Dickens, Charles Darwin and William Ewart Gladstone. By 1852, membership had doubled, with a 'lending circulation of about 40,000 volumes'. The intention was to be distinct from the more popular circulating libraries and to provide books 'people will read and continue to read'. Carlyle accordingly marked in the catalogues of other libraries the books he understood to be 'good'. Gladstone did the same for ecclesiastical history and Henry Hallam, whose *View of the State of Europe during the Middle Ages* was published in 1827, drew up lists of classical and medieval history and literature.[4] The printed catalogues of the London Library, which started in 1842 and were updated regularly throughout the nineteenth century, provide a good overview of which books met the committee's criteria. In some cases, they also note the price paid for the book and the bookseller.

For the crusades, they show that from the beginning, there was a good selection of histories, printed primary sources and more modern literature inspired by the crusades. They included works published outside Britain and in various European languages, such as Joseph François Michaud's *Histoire des croisades* (1811–22), the collection of sources *Bibliothèque des croisades* (1829) and in due course the *Recueil des historiens des croisades* (1844–1906). The library also had a copy of Heinrich von Sybel's *Geschichte des ersten kreuzzuge* (1841) and essays by Arnold Heeren (1808) and Maxime de Choiseul-Daillecourt (1808) on the influence of the crusades. By 1875, the catalogue included a classified index with an entry on crusade-related texts, and some twenty-seven were listed.

There are also records of the books borrowed by members. The ledgers (Issue books), from May 1841 to March 1849 and March 1856 to August 1858, have been preserved and list the dates of issue and return, titles and borrowers of books during this period. They are not easy reading because the quality of handwriting varies, and their very purpose meant that details of books returned were crossed through. Moreover, library practice changed during the 1840s. In the early volumes, the information is organised by date of issue, whereas in the later volumes, the arrangement is alphabetical, by author. The effort involved in deciphering the ledgers is, however, worthwhile.

What do they reveal? A handful of works on the subject of the crusades stand out as the most borrowed during the 1840s. One of these is *The Knights Templars* by Charles Greenstreet Addison, acquired in 1842 (Figure 1.1). Addison had travelled to the Holy Land and Syria on pilgrimage in the 1830s and published (in London and Philadelphia) an account of his journey and observations entitled *Damascus and Palmyra: A Journey to the East* in 1838, with illustrations by the novelist William Makepeace Thackeray, of whom more later. As a barrister in London, Addison was familiar with the Temple Church, which underwent major restoration in the 1840s. This, and his own visit to the Temple Mount in Jerusalem and other Templar sites, prompted him to write a history of the Templars, first published in 1842, and dedicated to the Benchers of the Inner and Middle Temples as well as the restorers of the church. He wrote:

> The proud and powerful Knights Templars were succeeded in the occupation of the Temple by a body of learned lawyers, who took possession of the old Hall and the gloomy cells of the military monks and converted the chief house of their order into the great

Figure 1.1 Frontispiece from Charles Addison's *History of the Knights Templar.* By permission of The London Library.

and most ancient Common Law University in England. For more than five centuries the retreats of the religious warriors have been devoted to 'the studious and eloquent pleaders of causes', a new kind of TEMPLARS, who, as Fuller [Thomas Fuller, author of *The Holy Warre,* 1639] quaintly observes, now 'defend one Christian from another, as the old ones did Christians from Pagans.[5]

The book was well received, running to several editions in which Addison expanded his history of the Order. He also produced a shorter book on the Temple church itself (1843).

Addison had firm views on his subject, challenging some of the 'more extraordinary and unfounded charges' levelled against the order:

> The vulgar notion that they were as wicked as they were fearless and brave, has not yet been entirely exploded; but it is hoped that the copious account of the proceedings against the order in this country given in the ensuing volume will dispel many unfounded prejudices still entertained against the fraternity, and excite emotions of admiration for their constancy and courage and or pity for their unmerited and cruel fate. [...] I have endeavoured to write a fair and impartial account of the order, not slavishly adopting everything I find in ancient writers, but such matters only, as I believe, after careful examination of the best authorities, to be true.[6]

The book also included a rather romanticised engraving of Templars in action, and it is still available today. Returning to his day job, Addison also produced two significant legal works, *A treatise on the law of torts* (1860) and *A treatise on the law of contracts* (1845).

Another regularly borrowed and rather different work was George Payne Rainsford James' history of the life of *Richard Coeur de Lion,* purchased for £2.2 shillings. James was a prolific author who turned out 'historical romances with industrial speed and efficiency'.[7] Appointed Historiographer Royal by William IV, in his later years, James combined his literary career with diplomacy, serving as British Consul in Norfolk, Virginia, and then the Adriatic before dying in Venice in 1860. James also had a wide range of acquaintances in both literary and political circles and was a friend and correspondent of Walter Scott, Gladstone and the Duke of Wellington.

His *Richard,* published in four volumes between 1842 and 1849, challenged the views of some contemporary crusade historians:

> The affected philanthropy and assumed liberality of some modern historians, have led them to represent the crusade as altogether cruel

and unnecessary; but so far from such being the case, it is evident that this warfare was [...] as just as any that was ever waged by man.[8]

James was also satirised by Thackeray in his *Barbazure* (as G.P.R. Jeaumes in *Novels by Eminent Hands* published in 1847) which has the warrior Philibert de Coquelicot declare:

> I stood by Richard of England at the gates of Ascalon, and drew the spear from the sainted King Louis in the tents of Damietta [...] I have broken a lance with Solyman at Rhodes and smoked a chibouque with Saladin at Acre.[9]

He also wrote a *History of Chivalry* (1843) and a three-volume novel about Richard I's French counterpart, *Philip Augustus* (1831).

Charles Mills, whose two-volume *History of the Crusades for the Recovery and Possession of the Holy Land* (published in 1820 and purchased by the Library in 1842 for fourteen shillings) was also regularly borrowed by library readers, was a more 'traditional' historian of the crusades. Another lawyer, his real interest was history, and his biographer, Augustine Skottowe, who may not have been the most objective witness, noted that 'no man was ever more punctilious in rigid investigation and statement of the facts'. Mills' intention certainly seems to have been to provide a balanced account of the crusades. His overall conclusion was that the crusading movement had:

> Retarded the march of civilization, thickened the clouds of ignorance and superstition; and encouraged intolerance, cruelty and fierceness [...] Painful is a retrospect of the consequences; but interesting are the historical details of the heroic and fanatical achievements of our ancestors [...] So visionary was the object, so apparently remote from selfish relations, that their fanaticism wears a character of generous virtue.[10]

Mills corresponded with Scott, who referred to the *History* in a footnote in *The Talisman*. Scott's novels, including the four set against the background of the crusades – *Ivanhoe* (1819), *The Betrothed* and *The Talisman* (1825) and *Count Robert of Paris* (1831) – were extensively borrowed by Library readers.[11] The Library also kept up to date with publications on the crusades, acquiring the histories written by Sir George Cox (in 1874) and Joseph Keightley (in 1847).[12] Readers were recorded as borrowing the accounts of those who had travelled to the East such as François-René de Chateaubriand, whose *Itineraire de Paris a Jerusalem* was published in 1811 and woven through with references to the crusades.[13] And there was also interest in foreign publications such as Abbe Vertot's history of the Hospitaller Order.

For many London Library readers, however, the abiding image or impression of the crusades probably came from the pen of the Italian poet Torquato Tasso, whose epic poem *Gerusalemme Liberata* was published in 1581. Set against the background of the First Crusade and, in his own era, the ongoing threat posed by the Ottoman Empire, Tasso combined the story of the capture of Jerusalem with the affair between the Christian knight Rinaldo and the Syrian enchantress Armida, the tragic love of the crusader Tancred for the Muslim maiden warrior Clorinda and the unrequited love of the pagan princess of Antioch, Erminia, for Tancred.

It was a much-read work, which Charles Brand[14] attributed to 'the Italianate fashion of the early nineteenth century which led any man of cultural pretensions and any young lady of social aspirations to learn Italian'. So it is not surprising that the Library has a number of editions of *Gerusalemme Liberata,* in both the original Italian and English translation, including Library member James Leigh Hunt's *Stories from the Italian Poets* published in 1846; the Issue books record that Hunt, a prominent English critic and writer, borrowed Tasso's works in December 1845. Hunt himself described *Gerusalemme* as a 'favourite epic of the young' and, even if its popularity may have declined in the latter half of the nineteenth century, eight English translations were produced between 1818 and 1865, and earlier translations, such as John Hoole's work of 1763, were recorded as being read by Samuel Johnson,[15] Walter Scott, William Wordsworth, Robert Southey and Thomas de Quincey.[16]

A translation of Tasso by Jeremiah Holmes Wiffen,[17] secretary and librarian to the Duke of Bedford at Woburn Abbey, was published in 1824 and was in the Library collection. It included a list of English Nobility and Gentry who went on the crusades, which may have interested Library readers eager to lay claim to their own crusading ancestors.[18] Wiffen's biographer (his daughter) wrote of her father's work: 'The pious heroism of the Champion of the First Crusade, Godfrey de Bouillon, as delineated by the Poet of the Cross, excited the admiration, and exercised an elevating influence, upon the spirit of the translator.'[19] She also quoted supporting references from Mills' *History of the Crusades.* In addition, Wiffen's edition included a number of woodcuts and, as I have discussed elsewhere,[20] scenes from the poem also inspired many contemporary artists and composers, with operas on this subject regularly performed in London and paintings exhibited at the Royal Academy annual exhibitions and in the collections of aristocratic houses throughout Britain. All of this must have added another layer of crusading imagery and memory.

Another well-known reader who was interested in the crusades was the novelist Thackeray, who borrowed the histories penned by Mills and Michaud in July 1845 (Figure 1.2). Thackeray published a novella, *Rebecca and Rowena*, in 1849, which continued the story of Scott's *Ivanhoe* and in his satire *Codlingsby* (1847) – Benjamin Disraeli's Young England novel *Coningsby* was published in 1844 – his Marquis is one Godfrey de Bouillon who regularly attends performances of Armida (the enchantress in Tasso's poem) at the theatre.

As already mentioned, Gladstone was an early member of the Library, and in spite of his many commitments he was a voracious reader, noting down in his diary the various books he had read, often with comments.[21] The edition of Gladstone's diaries by H.C.G. Matthew enables one to see what he read on the subject of the crusades, and a similar pattern emerges. Gladstone's own library also survives at St Deiniol's in Hawarden, Flintshire, and the online catalogue lists not only his books but also whether they have annotations and dedications.[22]

Like many contemporaries, Gladstone owned Tasso's *Gerusalemme* in various editions and translations and his diary recorded him reading the work in 1828, 1833, 1836 and 1853. His library included two

Figure 1.2 Extract from London Library Issue Book for July 1845. By permission of The London Library.

translations by Sir John Kingston James (the 1865 and 1884 editions), which were dedicated to Gladstone 'with profound respect and admiration'. James actually visited Jerusalem in 1863 and stood on the walls between the Jaffa and Damascus gates, 'Tasso in hand, realising the various incidents and localities mentioned in the immortal poem'. Gladstone also owned another nineteenth-century translation (1853) by a Captain A.C. Robertson of the 8th Hussars, who seems to have corresponded with Wordsworth about the challenges of the poetic metre.[23] Gladstone's own verdict, writing in his diary on 18 March 1836, was that the *Gerusalemme* was 'beautiful in its kind but how can the author be placed in the same category of genius with Dante'.

Gladstone of course may have been more interested in *Gerusalemme* as literature rather than an account, however fantastic, of the First Crusade, but there is other evidence of his interest in the crusades. As a pupil at Eton he had certainly read Mills' *History of the Crusades*, and he composed a poem of some 250 lines on Richard Coeur de Lion in 1827. It was published in the *Eton Miscellany,* a journal that Gladstone and his friend Arthur Hallam, son of the historian and writer Henry Hallam, founded. Gladstone also entered a poem on Richard for the Newdigate prize at Oxford in 1828. Rereading the work in later life, he was not much impressed with his youthful versification and did not agree to it being reprinted,[24] but it is a product of its time and one of Gladstone's friends, the classicist Joseph Anstice, won the prize that year.[25] Indeed, aspects of the crusades were chosen as the subject for the Newdigate prize on several occasions, and one critic wrote the following of Reginald Heber's 1803 poem Palestine:

> A more fertile field for the research of the antiquary, the learning of the scholar, the zeal of the Christian, and, the genius of the poet, was scarcely ever chosen, and we may safely and justly add that the execution is as successful as the selection was happy.[26]

Whilst at Eton, in 1826, Gladstone also recorded a lively debate between Hallam and another pupil about whether Richard I or Charles XII of Sweden was the 'finest character'. Hallam did not find Richard a character to admire:

> That Coeur de Lion was actuated by any religious feelings or any desire to recover the Holy Sepulchre from the grasp of an infidel, his actions, I think, do not give us any sufficient proof [...] I hold the atrocities of Richard to be of a deeper dye than those of the Swedish hero. Richard was a cast nigh-true chivalrous character

but like most of the heroes of those dark ages; was by turns generous and cruel, bigoted and unenlightened [...] irascible, haughty and vindictive.

Nevertheless, the members of the debating society voted for Richard by six votes to one.[27]

Arthur Hallam opens a window into further literary connections. With his father, he visited Walter Scott at Abbotsford in the summer of 1829, and at Cambridge he met the poet Alfred Tennyson, who wrote of crusade ancestors in two poems – *The Princess* and *Locksley Hall* – and whose uncle, Charles D'Eyncourt Tennyson, was involved in plans to found an English branch of the Order of the Temple in the 1830s.[28]

Gladstone also read other contemporaries' attempts at poems about crusades, such as Sir James Bland Burges' poem *Richard the First* which was published in 1801 (read in November 1878); Tommaso Grossi's *I Lombardi alla prima crociata* (read in 1826 and 1838) – a work which of course in turn inspired Verdi's nationalist opera *I Lombardi* (performed in London in 1846) – and William Stigand's *Athenais,* a romantic poem which was published in 1866 and read by him the following April.[29] Gladstone also read Addison on the Templars in 1842 (the year of its publication), noting that the Temple church 'is more striking on every visit'. His own library included a copy, with annotations and underlining, of the 1896 edition of Cox's *The Crusades.* Cox wrote of the crusaders as great actors in a wonderful drama but with mixed results:

> Worthless in themselves and wholly useless as a means for founding any permanent dominion in Palestine or elsewhere, these enterprises have affected the commonwealths of Europe in ways of which the promoters never dreamed. They left a wider gulf between the Greek and Latin churches, between the subjects of the eastern empire and the nations of western Europe; but by the mere fact of throwing east and west together they led gradually to that exchange of thought and that awakening of the human intellect to which we owe all that distinguishes our modern civilization from the religious and political systems of the middle ages.[30]

Gladstone enjoyed Scott's crusade novels, both as a young man in 1828, a few years after their publication, and in later life, commenting in 1860 that *The Talisman* 'is really fine' and 'I like it better than ever'. As a family, they read Scott to each other and Gladstone presented a set of Scott's novels to the Hawarden Institute. Although Scott became less fashionable as the century progressed, Gladstone remained a strong advocate of his ability to bring to life former ages, 'causing them to live and move before us, and us to live and move among them, as if we belonged to them and they belonged to us'.[31]

As well as the foundation of the London Library, the nineteenth century saw a number of other important developments in terms of access to books throughout Britain and for all classes of society. Whilst there was no public library system as such until after the Public Library Bill of 1850, books were accessible in a variety of ways.[32] Circulating libraries such as Mudie's, established by Charles Edward Mudie in 1842 and based in New Oxford Street in London, with over 87,000 works of history and biography added in just one year (1858–59), served a wide range of customers and offered a de-livery service outside the capital and overseas.[33] Libraries were also established in many towns and cities and the Mechanics' Institutes, set up to impart the elements of scientific education to working men, proved a much wider influence in promoting access to books, with 610 institutes by 1850 in England alone which owned some 700,000 volumes.[34] Richard Altick has written about 'the English common reader' and the library movement, noting that 'if millions read nothing but trash, scores of thousands, no wealthier and with no formal schooling, devoured serious fiction, poetry, essays, history, philosophy, theology and biography'.[35]

Louis James has also described the growth of popular literature published in periodicals and magazines and the role of Societies such as the Society for Promoting Christian Knowledge (SPCK) and the Society for the Diffusion of Christian Knowledge. They published many thousands of religious tracts, but they were also responsible for series designed to inform and educate a wide range of readers. Thus, Thomas Keightley's *The Crusaders or Scenes, Events and Characters from the Times of the Crusades* was published in 1833-34, under the direction of The Committee of General Literature and Education, appointed by the SPCK,[36] and Cox's *The Crusades* formed part of the series Epochs of Modern History, designed for history teaching in schools.

Again, published library catalogues give an indication of what was bought and borrowed on the subject of the crusades and it is a familiar list. For example, the Catalogue of the Stirling and Glasgow Public Library from 1888 included Addison's *History of the Templars* and editions and translations of Tasso. It also included histories of the crusades by Mills, Rev. Henry Stebbing (*History of Chivalry and the Crusades*, 1830) and Michaud. The 1843 catalogue of the London

Institution, founded in 1805, 'for the promotion of literature and useful knowledge' similarly had Tasso, Addison, James and Mills, although it is not clear whether, for a variety of reasons, they were in regular usage.[37] And in Manchester, Chetham's Library, founded in 1653 and regarded as the oldest public library in the English-speaking world, had seven editions of Tasso, as well as other crusade source texts. This selection of books is also consistent with the vision behind the development of libraries set out in the 1842 catalogue of Norfolk and Norwich Literary Institution founded as a subscription library in 1822:

> For the purpose of combining publications of the highest character, both English and foreign, in every department, with a liberal supply of the most interesting and popular literature of the day, and a general collection of standard works; thus whilst securing an ample provision of general amusement and information, its library of reference would present valuable and increasing faculties for the cultivation of literary and scientific pursuits.[38]

Here again Addison, James, Mills, Tasso and Scott were to be found on the library shelves, along with Vertot's *History of the Knights of Malta* and a seventeenth-century edition of Villehardouin's history of the Fourth Crusade.[39]

The catalogue of bookseller James Bohn, based at King William Street off The Strand in London, provides another insight into what was available. In 1840, Bohn offered for sale fourteen different editions or translations of Tasso, including an original 1581 edition from the library of Richard Heber, stepbrother of Reginald Heber and a noted book collector, histories of the crusades by Mills and Michaud and sources such as Joinville and Villehardouin.[40] His brother Henry Bohn also published editions of Joinville and Villehardouin in his Standard Library series.

A number of catalogues also survive of country house libraries, some still in situ such as the library of the Dukes of Devonshire at Chatsworth in Derbyshire; others sold and dispersed. And Mark Purcell's recently published study of the country house library notes that these books were used and read, rather than just shelved and admired:

> Despite the lures of field sports, muscular Christianity and imperial derring-do, many nineteenth century landowners were clearly actively engaged with their books. For some, indeed, they were among their most central preoccupations.[41]

Moreover, the books were accessed and consulted by visitors, and some houses such as Tyntesfield in Somerset even operated a lending library, keeping a register of borrowers.[42] The 1879 catalogue of the library at Chatsworth, reveals a remarkable collection of editions and translations of *Gerusalemme Liberata* (sixteen in all), many collected probably by the bibliophile sixth Duke (1790–1858). And the library also contained editions of Jean de Joinville's *Histoire de Saint Louis* and Louis Maimbourg's *Histoire des croisades*, published in 1676, as well as, of course, the complete novels of Walter Scott.[43] The Royal Collection also includes several editions of Tasso (in Italian and English translation). One of these editions is recorded as having been acquired by George III, when Prince of Wales, and several others appear to have been added to the collection by Queen Victoria. The Royal Collection also had editions of Michaud and Mills,[44] and Queen Victoria's journals reveal that she read and enjoyed Scott's *The Talisman* and *Ivanhoe*.[45]

The list of subscribers to Wiffen's Tasso, provides a further insight into aristocratic libraries, if not necessarily confirmed readers. It begins with King George IV; followed by the Prince of Denmark; various members of the British nobility; Walter Scott; the artists Sir Thomas Lawrence, David Wilkie, John Flaxman and architect Jeffrey Wyatt; together with a cross section of 'ordinary subscribers', who included several members of the Darby family, ironmasters of Coalbrookdale at the cutting edge of the Industrial Revolution and Robert Darwin, father of Charles Darwin. Wiffen also seems to have exchanged letters with a range of other scholars about his project.

Whilst not all of the contents of the libraries now owned by the National Trust are original to the houses, an online search of the collections shows the same 'favourites', such as Tasso and Scott, appearing consistently, as well as depictions of scenes from *Gerusalemme* by various artists.[46] Chirk Castle in Wales even has a portrait, probably of Robert Myddelton, dated *c*.1730, which shows him sitting at a table on which there is a volume inscribed 'Tasso'. Walter Scott's library at Abbotsford[47] followed a similar pattern, with copies of works by James, Mills (who, as previously mentioned, corresponded with Scott), Joinville, Villehardouin and the ubiquitous Tasso. Scott had several editions of the latter, in its original Italian as well as English translation, and in a letter dated 3 August 1824, he asked his publisher to pay his subscription to Wiffen's 'very beautiful' translation of Tasso, commenting that 'the translator has done justice to the poet and the artist to both'. In his novel *Waverley*, one of his characters also asked Waverley to help her with her translation of Tasso.[48]

Knowledge of books published in Britain and beyond was also spread through reviews in journals, particularly in the early nineteenth century, which seems to have been a boom time for such publications, which were widely accessible in public and private libraries. John Hayden's study of *The Romantic Reviewers, 1802–24* provides a survey of the range of journals that were available and the different perspectives they offered. Some of these publications would have included reviews on works relevant to the crusades; for example, the various translations of Tasso, which were reviewed widely in journals with very different standpoints, such as the *Westminster Review* and the *Eclectic Review*. Thus, a reviewer of Wiffen's translation in the former wrote that Tasso had 'produced a more lively impression than if he had even written a regular history of the crusades', whereas a reviewer in the latter in 1825 argued that Tasso gave 'a false view of the achievement which it celebrates'. Journals such as the *Gentleman's Magazine* also discussed in some detail new books such as Mills' *History of the Crusades*: 'a useful, compressed and well concatenated narrative of events which everybody wished to know and, when known, are not worth remembering' and recommended it 'as a proper and respectable companion to the historical collections in our libraries.[49] And a review in *The Christian Examiner and Church of Ireland Magazine* wrote the following of Keightley's history of the crusades:

> It is difficult to conceive a more interesting subject than that presented to us by Mr. Keightley; it abounds with research for the antiquary, picturesque for the romantic, speculation for the philosopher and events of undying interest for the historian; nor has poetry finer inventions, or fiction more striking situations than what sober fact can furnish from these eventful periods. We are not surprised that they became the theme of Tasso's song, and have indeed deeply tinged all modern history with their romantic dye.[50]

Journals also reviewed foreign publications about the crusades. So, there was clearly some debate, often lively, about different perspectives of the crusades amongst nineteenth-century British readers and critics.

Finally, the writings of some contemporaries provide an insight into their reading matter, either directly in diaries or in their fictional accounts of their characters' reading preferences. The novelist Elizabeth Gaskell wrote to a friend in the 1830s about books 'we have all read hundreds of times-Such as odd volumes of Hume, Shakespeare, Tasso'.[51] Tasso was also a favourite poet of the pioneer of the Gothic Novel, Ann

Radcliffe, who had two of her characters read his work in *The Italian* and *The Romance of the Forest*.[52] In her novel *Daniel Deronda*, published in 1876, George Eliot made her character Gwendoline declare 'I know nothing of Tasso, except the *Gerusalemme Liberata*, which we read and learnt by heart at school' and Daniel himself referred to his ancestor 'who had killed three Saracens in one encounter'. One literary scholar has in fact argued that the structure of *Daniel Deronda* is modelled on *Gerusalemme,* with the Christians as the heathens needing the Jews to liberate them, while the Jewess Mirah sings an aria from Handel's 1711 Tasso-derived opera Rinaldo.[53] Whether contemporary readers would have been aware of this is of course another matter.

What does one conclude from all this? First, the nineteenth-century reader had access to a wide range of works on the subject of the crusades from novels to poems, edited primary sources and histories. The growth of public and subscription libraries facilitated this access and reviews in journals and magazines would also have widened knowledge of works available. Some were clearly more popular than others, and popularity did not necessarily mean historical accuracy. The shadow cast by Tasso and Scott was very clear and significant in shaping the memory and perception of the crusading movement and its participants, both through the written word and pictorial image. The evidence is not available to draw any direct links between what some key figures such as Gladstone read and their handling of events in the East, but the records of their reading show some of the ways in which their cultural memory bank would have developed, drawing on contemporary crusade sources as well as the most imaginative fancies of poets and novelists.

Notes

1 See Paul Kaufman, *Libraries and Their Users: Collected Papers in Library History* (London,1969), pp. 11, 117, 144, and 218–19; Giles Mandelbrote and K. A. Manley, eds., *The Cambridge History of Libraries in Britain and Ireland*, vol. 2 (Cambridge, 2006); Jacqueline Pearson, *Women's Reading in Britain, 1750–1835* (Cambridge, 1999), pp. 162–63.
2 Mandelbrote and Manley, *Cambridge History,* 2, p. 2.
3 Frederic Harrison, ed., *Carlyle and the London Library* (London, 1907), pp. 8–11, 79–80 and 91; 'Signs of the Times' in *Scottish and Other Miscellanies* (London, 1839), p. 109. See also William Baker, *The Early History of the London Library* (Lampeter, 1992).
4 Ibid. pp. 57, 60–61, 65.
5 C. G. Addison, *The Temple Church* (London, 1843), p. 1.
6 Charles G. Addison, *History of the Knights Templar* (London, 1842), Preface and Chapter 1.

7 John Sutherland, *The Stanford Companion to Victorian Fiction* (Stanford, 1989). See also Stuart M. Ellis, *The Solitary Horseman or The Life and Adventures of G.P.R. James* (Kensington, 1927).

8 George P. R. James, *A History of the Life of Richard, Coeur de Lion, King of England,* 4 vols. (London, 1841), 1, p. 280.

9 George M. Thackeray, *Burlesques,* in *Novels by Eminent Hands* (London, 1900), p. 42.

10 Charles Mills, *History of the Crusades for the Recovery and Possession of the Holy Land,* 2 vols. (London, 1820), 1, pp. 373–74. Augustin Skottowe's biographical memoir was published in 1828, two years after Mills' death, by which time his *History* was in its fourth edition.

11 Scott's novels were also extensively read and copied in Europe. See Murray Pittock, ed., *The Reception of Walter Scott in Europe* (London, 2006).

12 For a survey of histories of the crusades published in Britain in the nineteenth century, see Siberry, *New Crusaders,* pp. 1–38 and Christopher Tyerman, *The Debate on the Crusades* (Manchester, 2011).

13 See Siberry, *New Crusaders,* pp. 51 and 68–69.

14 Charles P. Brand, *Torquato Tasso: A Study of the Poet and his Contribution to English Literature* (Cambridge, 1965), pp. 266–72.

15 Johnson's 1763 dedication of Hoole's translation was addressed to Queen Charlotte, wife of King George III, and drew links between the house of Hanover and Tasso's patrons, the house of Este. See Arthur Murphy, ed., *The Works of Samuel Johnson* (London, 1796), 2, p. 56.

16 *Oxford Guide to Literature in English Translation* (Oxford, 2000), pp. 482–83.

17 *Jerusalem Delivered,* trans. Jeremiah H. Wiffen, 2 vols. (London, 1824). See also *The Brothers Wiffen: Memoirs and Miscellanies,* ed. Samuel R. Pattison (London, 1880).

18 See Siberry, *New Crusaders,* pp. 39–64.

19 Pattison, *Brothers Wiffen,* p. 44.

20 Elizabeth Siberry, 'Tasso and the Crusades: History of a Legacy', *Journal of Medieval Studies* 19 (1993), pp. 163–69. The Oxford World's Classics' translation of Tasso's poem by Max Wickert (2009), pp. 400–403, includes a useful appendix listing examples of Tasso's influence in literature, art and music.

21 See Ruth Clayton Windscheffel, *Reading Gladstone* (London, 2008), who notes (p. 2) that, according to his diary, when he died in 1898, Gladstone had read approximately 20,000 titles written by over 4,500 authors and accumulated a library of over 30,000 items. Gladstone provided his servants with a library and visitors and local friends could also borrow his books (pp. 108–10 and 114).

22 *Gladstone's Library,* <www.gladstoneslibrary.org>, [accessed 11 August 2017]. For Gladstone's diary, see Henry C. G. Matthew, ed., *The Gladstone Diaries,* 14 vols. (Oxford, 1994).

23 Brand, *Tasso,* pp. 268–71.

24 John Morley, *The Life of William Ewart Gladstone* (London, 1903), p. 62.

25 *Oxford Prize Poems* (Oxford, 1831), pp. 212–24. Anstice's notes show that he had read Mills' *History of the Crusades.*

26 *The Monthly Mirror,* 16 (1803), pp. 38–39. Heber later became Bishop of Calcutta and the author of many hymns. Walter Scott, a family friend, is

said to have helped the student poet with his Newdigate entry (R. and A. S. Heber, *The Life of Reginald Heber* (London, 1830), p. 30), and it was later set to music by the composer William Crotch. In 1836, the Knights of St John were the subject of the Newdigate competition; followed by St Louis in 1873 and Richard I before Jerusalem in 1912.

27 Martin Blocksidge, *A Life Lived Quickly: Tennyson's Friend Arthur Hallam and His Legend* (Sussex, 2010), pp. 39–40, 47.

28 Hallam often visited the Tennyson family at Somersby in Lincolnshire and the nearby church of Harrington has an effigy of John de Harrington, who Tennyson describes as a crusader in his poem *Locksley Hall* (1886). For D'Eyncourt, see Mark Girouard, *The Return to Camelot: Chivalry and the English Gentleman* (New Haven, 1981), pp. 71–73; Siberry, *New Crusaders,* pp. 57–58 and Elizabeth Siberry, 'Victorian Perceptions of the Military Orders' in *The Military Orders: Fighting for the Faith and Caring for the Sick,* ed. Malcolm Barber (Ashgate, 1994), pp. 366–68.

29 On Stigand, see Elizabeth Siberry, 'Nineteenth Century Perspectives of the First Crusade' in *The Experience of Crusading,* eds. Marcus Bull and Norman Housley, vol. 1 (Cambridge, 2003), pp. 281–94.

30 George W. Cox, *The Crusades* (London, 1874), p. 216.

31 Clayton Windscheffel, *Reading Gladstone,* pp. 55, 65, 108–10 and 142. For other examples of the popularity of Scott, see *Cambridge History,* 2, pp. 513–14.

32 See Louis James, *Fiction for the Working Man, 1830–50* (Oxford, 1963), pp. 5–6 and Kaufman, *Libraries.*

33 Guinevere L. Griest, *Mudie's Circulating Library and the Victorian Novel* (Devon, 1970), pp. 38 and 238.

34 *Cambridge History,* 2, pp. 289–90 and 380–85.

35 Richard Altick, *The English Common Reader: A Social History of the Mass Reading Public 1800–1900,* 2nd edn. (Ohio, 1990), pp. 198, 226 and 240.

36 T. Keightley, *The Crusades: Scenes, Events and Characters from the Time of the Crusades* (London, 1833-4), p. 2, refers to Tasso and Wiffen's translation, noting that the poet:

37 K. A. Manley, 'E.B. Nicholson and the London Institution', *Journal of Librarianship* 5 (1973), pp. 52–77.

38 *Catalogue of the Norfolk and Norwich Literary Institution Systematically Arranged* (Norwich, 1842), p. v.

39 See also Kaufman, *Libraries,* pp. 117 and 144 for references to Tasso. Other catalogues which list crusade works in this period are the *Catalogue of the Central Lending Library Newcastle upon Tyne* (Newcastle, 1908) and *Catalogue of the Library of the Athenaeum Liverpool* (Liverpool, 1864). The latter contained some 20,000 books by 1864 and noted that 'members used Mudie's for modern books of a popular character'.

40 James Bohn, *Catalogue of Ancient and Modern Books in All Languages for Sale by James Bohn, no. 12 King William Street, Strand* (London, 1840).

41 Mark Purcell, *The Country House Library* (New Haven, CT, 2017), pp. 198–99.

42 Ibid., pp. 241–42.

43 James Lacaita, *Catalogue of Library at Chatsworth,* 4 vols. (London, 1879).

44 *Royal Collection Trust*, <www.royalcollection.org.uk>, [accessed 11 August 2017].
45 *Queen Victoria's Journals*, <www.queenvictoriasjournals.org>, [accessed 11 August 2017]. Scott's novels also inspired frescoes in the now demolished Garden Room at Buckingham Palace; see Siberry, *New Crusaders,* pp. 126–27.
46 *National Trust Collections*, <www.nationaltrustcollections.org.uk>, [accessed 11 August 2017].
47 John G. Cochrane, *The Catalogue of Library at Abbotsford* (Edinburgh, 1938). See also James Anderson, *Sir Walter Scott and History* (Edinburgh, 1981) and Siberry, *New Crusaders,* pp. 112–30.
48 H. J. C. Grierson, ed., *Letters of Sir Walter Scott*, 12 vols. (Edinburgh, 1935), 8, p. 343. See Robert Irwin, 'History, Fiction and Film: Islam Faces the Crusaders', in *Jerusalem the Golden: The Origins and Impact of the First Crusade,* eds. Susan Edgington and Luis Garcia-Guijarro (Turnhout, 2014), p. 351.
49 *Gentleman's Magazine,* 90 (1820), pp. 438–40, 523–25 and 609–13; *Eclectic Review,* 23 (1825), pp. 456–70; *Westminster Review* 12 (1826), pp. 404–45.
50 Review in 'Notices of books' in *The Christian Examiner and Church of Ireland Magazine* (1834), p. 54.
51 John Chapple, *Elizabeth Gaskell: The Early Years* (Manchester, 1997), p. 389. Gaskell also referred to the Fairfax translation of Tasso in her novel *North and South* (1854–55), (London, 1970), p. 257.
52 See Rictor Norton, *Mistress of Udolpho: The Life of Ann Radcliffe* (Leicester, 1999), p. 48 and Pearson, *Women's Reading,* pp. 100–105.
53 G. Eliot, *Daniel Deronda*, pp. 76 and 210; Barry Qualls, 'George Eliot and Religion' in *The Cambridge Companion to George Eliot,* ed. G. Levine (Cambridge, 2001), pp. 119–37. Eliot may have been more interested in the story of Tasso's life than his portrayal of the crusade. Her journal notes that she read Goethe's verse play 'Torquato Tasso' in Berlin in 1854 and saw some of Tasso's letters in the Ambrosian Library in Milan in 1860. See M. Harris and J. Johnston, eds. *The Journals of George Eliot* (Cambridge, 1998), pp. 38–40 and 366. Eliot also gave a character in her story *The Lifted Veil* (1859) the nickname Tasso (Oxford, 2009), p. 26.

Bibliography

Primary

Addison, Charles Greenstreet. *History of the Knights Templar.* London: Longman, 1842.
———. *The Temple Church.* London: Longman, 1843.
Carlyle, Thomas. *Scottish and other Miscellanies.* London: J.M. Dent, 1839.
Catalogue of Ancient and Modern Books in all languages for sale by James Bohn No. 12 King William Street, Strand. London: C. Richards, 1840.
Catalogue of the Library of the Athenaeum Liverpool. Liverpool: The Proprietors, 1864.

Catalogue of the Central Lending Library (excluding fiction in English, children's books and books for the blind), Newcastle upon Tyne. Newcastle upon Tyne: Andrew Dickson, 1908.

Catalogue of the Library of the London Institution, systematically classed. London: London Institution, 1835–43.

Catalogue of the Library of the Norfolk and Norwich Literary Institution, systematically arranged. Norwich: Norfolk and Norwich Literary Institution, 1842.

Catalogue of Stirling and Glasgow Public Library. Glasgow: R. Maclehose, 1888–97.

Cochrane, John G. *Catalogue of the Library at Abbotsford*. Edinburgh: Constable, 1938.

Cox, George William. *The Crusades*. London: Longman, Green and Co., 1874.

Ellis, Stuart Marsh. *The Solitary Horseman of The Life and Adventures of G.P.R. James*. Kensington, London: Cayme Press, 1927.

Harrison, Frederic. ed. *Carlyle and the London Library*. London: Chapman and Hall, 1907.

James, George Payne Rainsford. *A History of the Life of Richard Coeur de Lion, King of England*. London: H.G. Bohn, 1842.

Laciata, James. *Catalogue of the Library at Chatsworth*. 4 Vols. London: Chiswick Press, 1879.

Matthew, Henry C.G. *The Gladstone Diaries*. 14 Vols. Oxford: OUP, 1994.

Mills, Charles. *History of the Crusades*. London: Longman, 1820.

Morley, John. *The Life of William Ewart Gladstone*. London: Macmillan, 1903.

Murphy, Arthur. ed., *The Works of Samuel Johnson*. London: G. Walker, J. Akerman et al., 1796.

Oxford Prize Poems. 8th edn. Oxford: Parker, Vincent and Slatter, 1841.

Pattison, Samuel R. *The Brothers Wiffen: Memoirs and Miscellanies*. London: Hodder and Stoughton, 1880.

Purcell, Mark. *The Country House Library*. New Haven, CT: Yale, 2017.

Thackeray, George Makepeace. *Burlesques*. London: T. Nelson, 1900.

Wiffen, Jeremiah Holmes. *Jerusalem Delivered*. London: John Murray, 1824.

Secondary

Altick, Richard D. *The English Common Reader: A Social History of the Mass Reading Public 1800–1900*. Columbus, OH: State University Press, 1990.

Anderson, James. *Sir Walter Scott and History*. Edinburgh: Edina, 1981.

Baker, William. *The Early History of the London Library*. Lampeter: Mellen, 1992.

Black, Alistair and Peter Hoare. *The Cambridge History of Libraries in Britain and Ireland*. Vol. 3, 1850–2000. Cambridge: CUP, 2006.

Blocksidge, Martin. *A Life Lived Quickly: Tennyson's Friend Arthur Hallam and His Legend*. Sussex: Academic Press, 2010.

Brand, Charles. *Torquato Tasso: A Study of the Poet and his Contribution to English Literature*. Cambridge: CUP, 1995.

Chapple, John. *Elizabeth Gaskell: The Early Years*. Manchester: MUP, 1997.

Clayton Windscheffel, Ruth. *Reading Gladstone*. London: Palgrave Macmillan, 2008.

France, Peter. ed. *Oxford Guide to Literature in English Translation*. Oxford: OUP, 2001.

Girouard, Mark. *The Return to Camelot: Chivalry and the English Gentleman*. New Haven, CT: Yale, 1981.

Griest, Guinevere. *Mudie's Circulating Library and the Victorian Novel*. Devon: David and Charles, 1970.

Hayden, John. *The Romantic Reviewers, 1802–24*. Chicago: Chicago University Press, 1968.

Irwin, Robert. 'History, Fiction and Film: Islam faces the Crusaders'. In *Jerusalem the Golden: The Origins and Impact of the First Crusade*. eds. Susan Edgington and Luis Garcia-Guijarro. Turnhout: Brepols, 2014. pp. 347–71.

James, Louis. *Fiction for the Working Man: A Study of the Literature Produced for the Working Classes in Early Victorian England, 1830–50*. Oxford: OUP, 1963.

Kaufman, Paul. *Libraries and Their Users: Collected Papers in Library History*. London: Library Association, 1969.

Manley, K.A. 'E.B. Nicholson and the London Institution'. *Journal of Librarianship* 5 (1973), pp. 52–77.

Mandelbrote, Giles. and K.A. Manley. eds. *The Cambridge History of Libraries in Britain and Ireland*. Vol. 2, 1640–1850. Cambridge: CUP, 2006.

Norton, Rictor. *Mistress of Udolpho: The Life of Ann Radcliffe*. Leicester: Leicester University Press, 1999.

Pearson, Jacqueline.*Women's Reading in Britain, 1750–1835*. Cambridge: CUP, 1999.

Pittock, Murray, ed. *The Reception of Walter Scott in Europe*. London: Bloomsbury, 2006.

Qualls, Barry. 'George Eliot and Religion'. In *The Cambridge Companion to George Eliot*. ed. George Levine. Cambridge: CUP, 2001. pp. 119–37.

Siberry, Elizabeth. 'Tasso and the Crusades: History of a Legacy'. *Journal of Medieval History* 19 (1993), pp. 163–69.

———. 'Victorian Perceptions of the Military Orders'. In *The Military Orders: Fighting for Faith and Caring for the Sick*. ed. Malcolm. Barber. Aldershot: Ashgate, 1994. pp. 365–72.

———. *The New Crusaders: Images of the Crusades in the Nineteenth and Early Twentieth Centuries*. Aldershot: Ashgate, 2000.

———. 'Images and Perceptions of the Military Orders in Nineteenth Century Britain'. *Ordines Militares Colloquia Torunensia Historica* 11 (2001), pp. 197–210.

———. 'Nineteenth-Century Perspectives of the First Crusade'. In *The Experience of Crusading*. Vol. 1. eds. Marcus Bull and Norman Housley. Cambridge: CUP, 2003. pp. 281–94.

Sutherland, John. *The Stanford Companion to Victorian Fiction*. Stanford, CA: Stanford University Press, 1989.

Tyerman, Christopher. *The Debate on the Crusades*. Manchester: MUP, 2011.

Websites

Chetham's Library. www.library.chethams.com/catalogue. [Accessed 11 August 2017].

Gladstone's Library. www.gladstonelibrary.org. [Accessed 11 August 2017].

National Trust Collections. www.nationaltrustcollections.org.uk. [Accessed 11 August 2017].

Royal Collection Trust. www.royalcollection.org. [Accessed 11 August 2017].

Queen Victoria's Journals. www.queenvictoriasjournals.org. [Accessed 11 August 2017].

2 Creating chivalrous imperial crusaders

The crusades in juvenile literature from Scott to Newbolt, 1825–1917

Mike Horswell

The crusades and crusaders resonated with imperial Britons and were depicted with regularity in art and literature through the Victorian and Edwardian eras. Crusader medievalism occupied a central place in the nineteenth- and early twentieth-century British imaginary due to its ability to incorporate key cultural trends: it could serve the Romantic medieval revival, as well as aggressive imperialism and militant 'muscular' Christianity. This chapter will examine crusading fiction written by author-educators from 1825 to 1917 and demonstrate how the crusades served as a vehicle of enculturation for the empire's youth; crusader medievalism can be seen to have borne the weight of complementary attempts to educate young readers in what it meant to be a patriotic, chivalrous and pious Briton in the century leading up to the First World War.

Crusading fictions

The nineteenth century saw the rise in Britain of a cultural system that combined 'muscular' Christianity and imperial militarism with romantic medievalism to create an explicitly chivalric 'Christian gentlemen' who would serve the British Empire.[1] This culture enjoyed a symbiotic relationship with crusader medievalism: it provided a fertile environment for the appropriation of crusading rhetoric and imagery, and in return the crusades and crusading could be used to reinforce chivalric, imperial and contemporary Christian ideals. Children's literature was a key component of enculturation, or 'socialisation', whereby authors sought to inform and shape youth (particularly young men) according to the principles thought necessary for maintaining the British Empire and its heritage.[2] In engaging the imagination of a reader, Jacqueline Bratton has argued, fiction could speak directly to the individual ostensibly privately and at their discretion, making it a powerful tool of educators.[3]

In the mid-nineteenth century, the formative potential of literature was seized upon by Evangelical Christians who produced lessons in morality and stories of exemplary characters.[4] James Mangan has suggested that adventure fiction 'celebrated evangelical decency, the work ethic and imperial expansion' and that the middle-class Victorian boy was the primary (but not only) target for these values.[5] As the century progressed, the moralists were joined by imperialists seeking to promote the idea of the British Empire. Imperialist authors in the late nineteenth and early twentieth centuries:

> implicitly believed they were performing an important social function, doing their duty to Crown and Empire by preparing the youth of the nation to play their part in the inevitable struggles that would arise from Britain's imperial status and the jealousy of her rivals.[6]

Moreover, Anna Vaninskaya has observed, 'Victorian literary preferences, ensconced within a comprehensive ideologically didactic package, continued to structure primary educational provision well into the interwar period.'[7]

As Elizabeth Siberry has demonstrated, crusading had a significant cultural presence in the nineteenth century in poetry, art, music and plays (not least inspired by the popularity of Tasso's *Gerusalemme liberate* of 1581).[8] Crusading fictions formed a part of this literary landscape. They appear to have originated with Sophie Cottin's *Matilda and Malek Adhel*, translated from French and published in London in 1809.[9] The author was acquainted with the French crusade historian Joseph François Michaud, who wrote the historical preface for the first edition of her novel.[10] Two other crusading novels also predated 1825: Louisa Stanhope's *The Crusaders* (1820) and Barbara Hofland's *Theodore* (1821).[11] Without including Sir Walter Scott's novels, Felix Hinz has identified thirty-seven crusading novels published in English before the First World War – every major crusade was represented up to that of Edward I in the 1270s.[12] Indeed, an 'almost obligatory crusade ancestor' was a staple of fictional aristocracy throughout the century.[13]

In his evaluation of juvenile literature written about the Holy Land between 1785 and 1940, Joseph Shadur has identified the crusades as a distinct topic of interest. Books for children on the Holy Land largely began appearing with Napoleon's invasion of Egypt in 1798, but their numbers increased in the 1820s and represented a 'steady stream' thereafter.[14] Of the books specifically dealing with the crusades, Shadur has summarised that:

> Notwithstanding the inherent anti-Catholicism of most of the writers, in all these works the old Catholic view of devout, heroic, chivalrous Christian dedication to the 'liberation' of the Holy Sepulcher and other Christian holy sites from Muslim desecration is resuscitated and held up as an absolute, overriding ideal – right throughout World War I and thereafter. The British troops fighting the Turks in Palestine in 1917–18, were commonly seen as modern Crusaders battling the Saracens.[15]

Similarly, Velma Richmond's study of chivalric stories for children published in Edwardian-era anthologies in Britain has found many examples of crusading tales, in which Richard the Lionheart featured prominently.[16] Siberry concluded her survey of crusade imagery in literature with the observation that:

> The standard formulae seem to have been employed, from the absent and returning crusader to the romanticized crusade hero, fictional or historically based, in particular Richard I and, as ever, [Torquato] Tasso and Scott were the key sources of imagery and influence.[17]

Stories about the crusades were a way for authors and their readers to engage with the nature and impact of imperialism both at home and abroad. Megan Morris has explained that:

> Because chivalry and the crusades play a key role in the nineteenth-century social and moral imagination, nineteenth-century representations of the crusades are central to understanding nineteenth-century medievalism and its broader social impact. [...] These works, whether romantic or satirical, employ the motif of crusading to engage with a wide range of issues that are of central concern to students of nineteenth-century medievalism: nationalism, imperialism, domesticity, race, gender, and chivalry.[18]

Crusading fiction, therefore, was illustrative of the significant imaginative investment made by Victorian and Edwardian Britain in crusader medievalism, whilst reinforcing its close association.

Standing behind many of the nineteenth-century depictions of the crusades in British culture were Scott's crusading novels; his vision of the crusades and their participants hugely influenced subsequent generations and he was read by school children in English textbooks and readers up to the start of the twentieth century.[19] The broad scope of Scott's impact in popularising both medievalism and chivalry in the nineteenth century has been established, while Siberry has investigated Scott's engagement with the crusades in detail.[20]

Of his 'crusader' novels, *The Talisman* (1825) most directly involved the crusades as it was set at the end of the twelfth century during the Third Crusade (1189–92).[21] Regarding King Richard I of England and his counterpoint, the Muslim leader Saladin, Scott famously wrote:

> the warlike character of Richard I., wild and generous, a pattern of chivalry, [...] was opposed to that of Saladin, in which the Christian and English monarch showed all the cruelty and violence of an Eastern sultan, and Saladin, on the other hand, displayed the deep policy and prudence of a European sovereign, whilst each contended which should excel the other in the knightly qualities of bravery and generosity.[22]

Scott was 'much more interested in the dynamics of contact and encounter between East and West' than any actual Christian-Muslim conflict.[23] Antagonism, the author suggested, had been 'softened' by the cross-cultural contact which had transmitted chivalry to the Saracens.[24] Commentators have found in this transfer a proposed alternate victory for the crusade (absent from history) and a model for the imperial project. Authors such as Cottin had used that conversion to Christianity to bring a triumphant revisionist closure to the crusade; Scott, however, had Saladin make it clear that conversion was unthinkable, thereby rejecting a religiously orientated narrative.[25] In lieu of a religious war, or even an East-West conflict, the Third Crusade in *The Talisman* was overwritten by the demands of Scott's narrative of chivalric encounter.[26] Morris therefore concluded:

> Crusading thus plays a curious role within the text. While it motivates the ideological zeal that precipitates conflicts between Christian and Muslim knights, the physical act of chivalric battle simultaneously erases these ideological distinctions. [...] If virtuous Muslim and Christian knights are essentially the same, there is no need for them to battle one another.[27]

The Talisman, then, functioned as a discussion of chivalry set in the historical Third Crusade, in which Scott, though the trials of the fictional protagonist Kenneth, played out the incompatibilities and tensions of chivalric loyalty and duty to sovereign, faith and lady which provided the drama of the tale. The crusade was a fitting backdrop for an exploration of chivalric virtue.

For Scott, as his essay on chivalry in the *Encyclopædia Britannica* related, the crusade endeavour was essentially 'founded on the spirit of chivalry.'[28] The defence of Malta by the Hospitallers, central to his last novel *The Siege of Malta*, attracted Scott because it could be considered the final act of chivalry; there he found 'the Spirit of Chivalry blazing in its ashes.'[29] The huge popularity of Scott's historical fiction ensured that his characterisations of historical personages and of the crusades as a chivalrous drama were appropriated and rearticulated in countless forms: 'chivalry and the crusades became all but synonymous in the nineteenth-century British and American popular consciousness.'[30] Scott popularised chivalrous uses for the crusades, demonstrating their dramatic potential and contributing to the process whereby chivalry became an important pillar of British imperial identity.[31]

The following sections will consider the ways in which three authors of juvenile fiction combined their strong educational interests with tales set in and around various crusades. They spanned the era under consideration, overlapping with one another through the Victorian and Edwardian periods to the First World War. Charlotte M. Yonge (1823–1901), a lifelong fan of Scott, wrote moralistic stories for young people in the mid-nineteenth century while the phenomenally popular George A. Henty (1832–1902) wrote imperialist adventure fiction in the boom years of juvenile literature at the turn of the century. A generation later, Sir Henry Newbolt's (1862–1938) version of a glorious and chivalric thread of national history was expressed in his fiction and the patriotic verse he was better known for – and in his vision for an English curriculum. All three were interested in historical events, and all were invested in the education of British youth; evaluating their crusading works illustrates how crusader medievalism could function as a palimpsest for contemporary concerns.

Duty unto death: Charlotte M. Yonge

Noted for her involvement in the Anglo-Catholic Tractarian movement, Yonge was a novelist, textbook writer, critic and editor best known for *The Heir of Redclyffe* (1853). Educated by her father and concerned throughout her life with teaching in the village Sunday school, Yonge edited a magazine for girls, *The Monthly Packet*, between 1851 and 1894 and produced influential readers for schools in literature and history.[32] Yonge wrote over 200 works and was 'one of the best-selling woman writers of the Victorian period.'[33] Her influence was 'pervasive', especially through the wide distribution of the various textbooks she authored; she was heralded as the 'mother of historical fiction for children' by one historian.[34] Yonge, like other mid-Victorian writers, took seriously the potential for her work to form her readers. Her fiction has been characterised as both 'scrupulously moral agonizing' and 'the rehearsal rooms for productions of patriotic English men.'[35] History was seen to address concerns of morality, nationalism and masculinity because of the didactic potential of the exposure of young readers to societies of the past.

Yonge's crusading novel, *The Prince and the Page*, was published in 1866 and set in the crusade of Prince (later King) Edward of England (1270–72). The story followed Richard de Montfort as he was discovered by Prince Edward, recruited to be his page, and accompanied Edward on his crusade. The characters travelled to Tunis and the Holy Land, and mention was made of unsuccessful previous crusades. However, no explanation was given as to why Edward had vowed to fight in the Holy Land, only that he had and was determined to arrive there.[36] In conversation with his errant brother Simon, Richard refused to join Simon's independent holding in Galilee because he was 'a sworn crusader'; his renegade brother retorted: 'what are we but crusaders too, boy? 'Tis all service against the Moslem!'[37] Crusading was understood to have been a vaguely 'sacred' endeavour against Muslim enemies with Jerusalem an offstage aim.[38]

The preface to the book stated Yonge's educational hope of promoting 'sympathy and appreciation' of the 'great characters of our early annals.'[39] The great character of her book was Edward, whom Yonge called 'the English Justinian.' After the first couple of chapters Richard devotedly followed him as his page and the text repeatedly eulogised Edward as a chivalrous leader ahead of his time.[40] Edward consistently sought reconciliation with Richard's family despite provocation and exercised justice impartially when Richard's honour was in doubt. As with other of Yonge's tales, *The Prince and the Page* had at its heart family dynamics. Before the start of the story Richard's father and brothers had led a failed rebellion against Edward's father. Richard's oldest brother Henry, presumed dead, was discovered living as a beggar with Hospitaller Knights in London, whilst the antagonist of the novel was Simon, whose actions repeatedly placed Richard under suspicion from Edward's court. At the climax of the tale Simon attempted to kill Edward when he stayed with the Hospitallers in Acre, but by mistake fatally stabbed Richard instead. Richard's dying wish was the reconciliation of the Prince and his brother, which his shocked brother agreed to.[41] Richard's sacrifice for Edward saved his life and signified the preservation of the future of the nation (in the form of the Prince's person), as well as the resolution of the baronial civil war, which Richard's fractured family embodied.[42]

Yonge attempted to 'redefine both chivalry and crusade in accordance with nineteenth-century domestic virtues'; including a Christian moral code.[43] While the external events of the crusade caused Richard little trouble, the novel dwelt on his three opportunities for escaping from the uncertain outcomes of due process when he was accused (falsely) of wrongdoing. This conformed with Yonge's aim of history writing: 'as feebly tracing the dealings of God with mankind; and at the same time, as a religious lesson, a course of examples and warnings, calculated, alike by greatness and reality, to impress the mind.'[44] The crusade of Edward served as the historical setting for the exemplary tale of heroism and courage which culminated in the Christ-like 'martyrdom' of Richard. Richard's death for Edward – the ultimate act of national service – illustrated Yonge's ideal of chivalric heroism being both a Christian act of self-sacrifice for others and a patriotic duty unto death.

We see, then, how the influence of Scott's chivalrous crusading and the 'great man' view of history could come together to produce narratives centred on heroes who served as moral teaching aids. The crusades themselves provided 'glorious', if underdeveloped, background scenery for the national figures and the domestic morality with which Yonge was primarily concerned. A complex mix of chivalrous Christian morality and patriotic nationalism shaped perceptions of historical personages and of events through *The Prince and the Page*. Where Edward embodied the nation of England (upon which readers would have understood their Britain to stand in continuity), Richard represented a character for the young audience to identify with and emulate in his moral dilemmas and ultimate self-sacrifice. Yonge's work reveals the amalgam of national, moral and Christian concerns of the author as they were transmitted to her audience using a crusading setting and narrative. Later nineteenth-century juvenile literature moved away from evangelical didacticism and instead mobilised the potential of adventure fiction for imperial purposes.[45]

'War in its most picturesque form': George A. Henty[46]

Henty was known on both sides of the Atlantic for his adventure stories for boys: his prodigious output consisted almost entirely of war stories, roughly half of which were set in the past.[47] Before he took up novel-writing Henty had served in the British army and travelled widely as a war correspondent, notably in the Crimean War, and was involved with two magazines for boys – the *Union Jack* (1880–83) and *Beeton's Boys' Own Magazine* (1888–90). He was estimated to have sold three-and-a-half-million books in the UK alone through his publisher, Blackie, and potentially twenty-five million books worldwide.[48] The goals of education and entertainment were not assumed by Henty to be mutually exclusive: 'it being my object now, as always,' he wrote, 'to amuse, as well as to give instruction in the facts of history.'[49] Henty's biographer G. M. Fenn claimed that he 'taught more lasting history to boys than all the schoolmasters of his generation.'[50] He was explicit about the type of education he aimed to give; 'my object has been to teach history and still more to encourage manly and straight living and feeling amongst boys.'[51] Henty, therefore, consulted works of history to inform his novels and was, in turn, widely used in classrooms across Europe.[52]

In evaluating the impact of juvenile literature leading up to the First World War, Michael Paris has argued that Henty played a key role in romanticising warfare to appeal to young men and boys, 'in order to inculcate a sense of duty in his readers and the commitment to defend the empire.'[53] This depiction was 'an idealised portrait of the imperial warrior' which combined aspects of imperial representation (stereotypical racial characteristics, colonial settings, British superiority) and 'chivalric manliness' with fast-paced adventure stories which enacted Henty's vision of vigorous boyhood.[54] Jerome de Groot called Henty 'an apologist for empire', while he was, one contemporary remarked, 'the most Imperialist of all the Imperialists I have encountered.'[55]

In Henty's *Winning His Spurs* (1882), the hero, a young English noble called Cuthbert, followed King Richard I through the course of the Third Crusade. The non-stop account of historical adventure-tourism was unrelenting and missed no occasion to exploit either the historical setting or crusade-specific opportunities for action. Cuthbert fought alongside outlawed archers from Evesham forest, joined the crusaders' mustering in France and Sicily, won distinction and his knighthood fighting for Richard in Palestine, was captured and taken to Jerusalem, was nearly hanged, rescued his promised bride, found the imprisoned Richard and finally married and settled in his newly acquired estate in Evesham. In a nod to Scott, Cuthbert met a mysterious hermit in the desert during one adventure; as in *The Talisman*, the hermit turned out to be an ex-French knight with a hidden room in his cave.[56] Very few staples of imperial adventure novels were absent: Cuthbert was captured, visited a harem, escaped (twice) disguised as an Arab and was instrumental in the successes of the crusade by both might and ingenuity.[57]

Analytical lenses of gender, class and race distinctly reveal the structure of Henty's medieval world. The passivity of the female characters was notable: Cuthbert rescued his mother, future bride Margaret (twice) and Richard's fiancée during the novel.[58] The earthy outlaws recognised Cuthbert's innate nobility and followed him loyally through his travels; Cuthbert, in turn, served his lord, Sir Walter of Evesham, and King Richard faithfully. His chief retainer, Cnut, was of Saxon stock and entirely subject to his emotions. Cuthbert compared him to an unrestrained animal: 'Cnut had something of the nature of a bull in him. There are certain things which he cannot stomach, and when he seeth them he rageth like a wild beast, regardless altogether of safety or convenience.'[59] Furthermore, the racial composition of England echoed Scott's division of Saxon serfs and Norman overlords in *Ivanhoe*, except that the hope was expressed that the crusade would bring the two together:

> methinks that when the Saxon and the Norman stand side by side on the soil of the Holy Land, and shout together for England, it must needs bind them together, and lead them to feel that they are no longer Normans and Saxons, but Englishmen.[60]

As in Yonge's work, the events of the crusade potentially provided a site for national healing and strengthening of a united British identity. 'In Henty, then,' Robert Irwin concluded, 'going on crusades is not merely character-forming, but nation-forming.'[61]

Henty's medievalism was one of an ordered society: female characters were passive and needed rescuing, the outlaws and lower classes respected the 'natural authority' of nobility and the emergent English/British top of the racial hierarchy. Though there was significant potential within the crusade for social disruption and reordering – glimpsed in the quote regarding the possibility of the forging of a new national identity above – this was enacted only for Cuthbert, who took his opportunities for glory to earn knighthood from the hands of King Richard. Cuthbert began the story in the forest with the outlaws and ended it married and securely installed as the Earl of Evesham. There was no mention of Richard's death – he was last seen presiding over Cuthbert's wedding. These aspects of female passivity, assignment of racial traits and class harmony (when rightly ordered) provided the fabric of Henty's conservative medievalism, which was mixed with Cuthbert's coming-of-age tale.

Unlike Yonge, Henty did address the causes and purpose of the crusade, although in a double manner. In a dialogue between Cuthbert and Father Francis, a local priest who preached the crusade in Evesham, the religious justification and dynamics of the crusade were articulated. The First Crusade was presented as a response to Muslim persecution of Christian pilgrims; the expedition, Francis related, was encouraged by Pope Urban.[62] The religious reasons given for the crusade, however, were contradicted by Henty's own authorial interjection at the point when Cuthbert departed:

> It must not be supposed that the whole of those present were animated by any strong religious feeling. No doubt there existed a desire, which was carefully fanned by the preaching of the priests and monks, to rescue the holy sepulcher from the hands of the Saracens; but a far stronger feeling was to be found in the warlike nature of the people in those days. Knights, men-at-arms, and indeed men of all ranks, were full of a combative spirit. Life in the castle and hut was alike dull and monotonous, and the excitement of war and adventure was greatly looked for both as a means of obtaining glory and booty; and for the change they afforded to the dreary monotony of life.[63]

For Henty, then, the crusades were, despite the religious rhetoric, an opportunity for adventure and escape from the boredom of everyday life. Indeed, medieval war was 'picturesque': 'This was indeed war in its most picturesque form, a form which, as far as beauty is concerned, has been altogether altered, and indeed destroyed, by modern arms.' Unlike contemporary warfare, Henty asserted, 'prowess and bravery went for everything' and 'battles were decided as much by the prowess and bravery of the leader and his immediate following as by that of the great mass of the army.'[64]

Henty's view of the Third Crusade, and crusading, can therefore be seen to be 'picturesque': a form of warfare in which deeds of heroism stood out and in which individuals could make their fortune. Both Yonge and Henty's heroes had fictional adventures amongst real historical personages for whom crusading provided a background for adventure. As his books dealt with British and proto-British heroes and heroines through the ages, Henty created a continuum of recognisable national heroism which stretched from Roman times to the imperial present. The hero of *Winning His Spurs* modelled the characteristics of action, ingenuity and chivalric comportment as part of an ordered society. Henty's massive popularity and educational inclination, coupled with his unabashed imperialism, drove his version of a coming-of-age crusading tale in the context of a continuity of British heroism and manly pluck. As Cuthbert's extensive travels showed, Henty exercised the potential for escapist imperial tourism to the fullest extent he could, making sure he left the world intact behind him.

'A past which can never be truly spoken of as dead': Sir Henry Newbolt[65]

The less secure years of the First World War brought a clearer articulation of the continuity of British chivalric history with the work of Sir Henry Newbolt. Most famous now for his ellipsis of battle and cricket in the poem 'Vitae Lampada', Newbolt was a prominent imperial poet, educationalist and author of historical fiction at the turn of the century. The line 'Play up! Play up and play the game!' from the above work came to represent the imperial ethos which considered public school games as the training ground for service in colonial fields.[66] Indeed, Newbolt's 'The Vigil' was printed on the front page of *The Times* the day war with Germany was declared in 1914. Such was the positive reception that Newbolt was knighted, though he later had an ambiguous relationship with the famous line.[67] Having achieved fame for his patriotic poems Newbolt worked during the First World War for the Admiralty, Foreign Office and the Ministry of Information attached to Wellington House. Following the war, he was made Educational Editor for Nelson publishers by fellow wartime propagandist and author John Buchan, and subsequently chaired the Board of Education committee which produced the influential 1921 Newbolt Report that lobbied for the place of English in a national curriculum.[68] Newbolt was an educator with the ear of the government in the early twentieth century whose views were influential in forming a national education for young people.

During the first decades of the twentieth century Newbolt took up writing. Aiming his fiction at boys, he wrote adventure stories with the intention to inspire his readers to emulate their heroes' deeds. *The Book of the Happy Warrior* was published towards the end of the First World War in 1917 and was an attempt to bring chivalric heroes to the attention of boys in Britain.[69] The book consisted of chapters relating to various medieval heroes, which Newbolt had either written himself or translated, and concluded with two chapters explaining how the public schools of his day were the torch-bearers of the traditions of medieval knights.[70] The didactic aims of the book were twofold. Newbolt explicitly held up models of chivalry worthy of imitation whilst demonstrating that chivalry was an essential component of modern life and warfare. *The Book of the Happy Warrior* can be understood as a textbook – by presenting classic examples of chivalric heroes to students Newbolt's book functioned as a 'reader' in chivalry.[71] It also bore the marks of its wartime construction as all the examples of heroism presented were British or French – Germanic chivalry had been expunged.[72]

It is within this framework that Newbolt presented his heroes. After a chapter which dealt with the *Chanson de Roland*, the second chapter focussed on King Richard the Lionheart who was depicted as being motivated by 'desire for war and pilgrimage'. In the passage Newbolt translated, Richard was shown to be a terrifying opponent for the Turks, many of whom he slaughtered, and an inspiring leader of troops who encouraged his men in a dire situation that 'there is nothing that cannot be borne by a manly heart [...]; it is a man's choice, to win bravely or die with honour.'[73] Richard's decidedly unchivalrous decision to execute the garrison of Acre after its surrender to him in August 1191 was omitted; instead the English king was heralded for his prowess in battle and seen slicing through enemies with impunity.[74] Crusading, as embodied by Richard in this depiction, was seen to be an uncomplicated exercise in 'manly' Turk-bashing.

The next chapter which directly related to the crusades was another translation, this time from John of Joinville's account of St. Louis' expedition to Egypt in 1248. Louis successfully took the city of Damietta before his army was destroyed and he was himself taken captive. His chivalric character was witnessed in his scrupulous honesty – even in defeat he corrected the Saracens when they miscounted the amount paid in one instalment for his ransom in his favour.[75] Again, there was no mention of Louis' later expedition to Tunis where he died of illness in 1270. Subsequent chapters offered further insight into Newbolt's perception of the past. His account of Robin Hood was that of the natural bonds of loyalty and affection between yeoman and king being disrupted by grasping lords and the king's attempt to have Robin live at court. Chapters on an England versus France jousting tournament (in which the English knights sportingly recognised the superiority of the French), the deeds of Edward the Black Prince, Betrand du Guesclin and Bayard all contributed knightly examples of chivalric behaviour. Indeed, Bayard was notable for being almost entirely overdetermined by his designation as a paragon of chivalry.[76]

Newbolt's understanding of the past was most clearly revealed in a chapter taken from his novel *The Old Country* (1906), in which an early twentieth-century youth named Stephen Bulmer accidentally travelled back in time to the fourteenth century.[77] There, medieval characters taught Stephen the nature and value of chivalry. Chivalry was presented as the practical solution to the tension between Christian ideals and the trials of the real world: 'You make Christianity, in short, a counsel of perfection, to be postponed indefinitely?' asked Bulmer of the medieval Lord Bryan, who replied 'We should do so but for Chivalry.'[78] As Newbolt's preface to the chapter related, Stephen was 'more struck by the similarity between the thought of the fourteenth and twentieth centuries than by the external and trivial differences'.[79]

It was this continuity that was the key component of Newbolt's patriotism, also expressed in his poetry; 'the essential similarity of past and present' enabled the construction of a continuing heroic tradition which was distinctively English, and essentially chivalric.[80] 'A past', Newbolt wrote in his dedication at the beginning of *The Old Country*, 'which can never be truly spoken of as dead.'[81] This perception of continuity informed Newbolt's educational ethos and explained his inclusion in *The Book of the Happy Warrior* of the history of the public school system through the centuries as a demonstration and defence of this continuing tradition. Newbolt's patriotism and value of this tradition both stemmed from seeing the past as a living continuum to learn from and be inspired by. *The Book of the Happy Warrior* could, therefore, congruously identify chivalry and British heroism in both the British Army during the First World War and in Richard I during the Third Crusade.[82] Furthermore, this enabled Newbolt to proclaim in 1916 that British airmen were like chivalrous knights whose combat was the modern equivalent of jousting.[83]

The crusades, for Newbolt, provided sites – 'tournament fields' – for acts of chivalry, serving as the backdrop for exemplary, inspirational heroes, such as Richard I, who were part of an accessible past in conversation with the present. Newbolt saw the crusades as figuring centrally in the continuing story of Britain; his 'great men' were defined by their chivalry which in turn was a practical expression of Christianity. In *The Book of the Happy Warrior* (the title itself a reference to a poem by William Wordsworth) Newbolt created a corpus of chivalric exemplar, part of a national tradition which animated patriotism and demanded its continuation in wartime Britain.

Conclusion

Significant authors for a century after Scott included crusading novels in their *oeuvre*. The careers of the three writers considered above spanned the Victorian and Edwardian eras. Their concern to educate and edify their young audiences, typical of authors in this period, was expressed in both the content of their writings and in their direct participation in setting the educational agenda for schools; whether through writing or editing textbooks, or in Newbolt's case chairing a government committee. And all three saw in the crusades a rich and potent resource through which to educate young Britons.

The authors' perceptions and use of crusading examined here conformed to and actively helped to inculcate and perpetuate the cultural system Mark Girouard argued came to dominate the British upper classes in the late nineteenth century. Crusading could provide a backdrop for the ideals these authors sought to educate British youth in; the crusades were perceived to have combined Christian piety and militarism with individual prowess and heroism, lending themselves to the cult of chivalry which had so moved Britain's elite. In the context of an increasingly militarised British culture, images of crusaders and the crusades could stand centrally for the cultural amalgam of Christianity, imperial militarism and a romantic medievalism which produced a particularly British form of chivalry.

Each of the works examined above bear features of its time. In keeping with the Evangelical desire for moral exemplars, Yonge's hero died a Christ-like sacrificial death. This was concurrently a patriotic act as it preserved the royal heir and enacted restoration of national unity through the reconciliation of Richard's rebellious family. Amidst the context of a confident, global and militantly expansive British Empire, Henty's heroic adventure-tourism modelled the active, ingenious and chivalric life befitting an imperial youth's passage to settled maturity and the potential for warfare to facilitate this. Cuthbert, as with so many of Henty's heroes, embodied a journey from obscurity to upholding the fabric of society. Newbolt advocated a continuing national, chivalric tradition which had been preserved in the public school system and best represented a practical Christianity. Writing during the upheaval of the First World War, Newbolt strove to call up the nation's youth to express elements of the national character which would preserve the nation. He sought to reinforce British resolve through the invocation of an enduring continuity of British chivalry. All three saw the medieval past in general, and the crusades in particular, as an appropriate palimpsest for didactic enterprises, variously Christian, imperial and chivalric.

Notes

1 Mark Girouard, *Return to Camelot* (London, 1981), pp. 7–28.
2 See Michael Paris, *Over the Top: The Great War and Juvenile Literature in Britain* (London, 2004), p. xv; John M. MacKenzie, *Propaganda and Empire: The Manipulation of British Public Opinion 1880–1960* (Manchester, 1990), pp. 198–226.
3 Jacqueline S. Bratton, 'Of England, Home and Duty: The Image of England in Victorian and Edwardian Juvenile Fiction' in *Imperialism and Popular Culture*, ed. John M. MacKenzie (Manchester, 1986), p. 76.
4 Michael Paris, *Warrior Nation* (London, 2000), p. 50.
5 James A. Mangan, 'Noble Specimens of Manhood: Schoolboy Literature and the Creation of a Colonial Chivalric Code', *The International Journal of the History of Sport* 27 (2010), p. 389.
6 Paris, *Over the Top*, p. xviii.
7 Anna Vaninskaya, 'English Literature', *Journal of Victorian Culture* 12 (2007), p. 279.
8 Siberry, *New Crusaders*, pp. 131–87; Elizabeth Siberry, 'Tasso and the Crusades: History of a Legacy', *Journal of Medieval History* 19 (1993), pp. 163–69.
9 Sophie Cottin, *Matilda and Malek Adhel, the Saracen* (London, 1809).
10 Siberry, *New Crusaders*, p. 148.
11 Louisa Sidney Stanhope, *The Crusaders: An Historical Romance of the Twelfth Century* (London, 1820); Barbara Hofland, *Theodore, or The Crusaders: A Tale for Youth* (London, 1921). Andrew Lincoln also notes Eleanor Anne Porden's epic poem *Coeur de Lion* from 1822 as an important precursor to Scott; Andrew Lincoln, *Walter Scott and Modernity* (Edinburgh, 2007), p. 107.
12 Felix Hinz, *Kreuzzüge des Mittelalters und der Neuzeit* (Hildesheim, 2015), pp. 347–58; Siberry, *New Crusaders*, pp. 153–59.
13 Ibid., pp. 39–63 at p. 57.
14 Joseph Shadur, *Young Travelers to Jerusalem: The Holy Land in American and English Juvenile Literature, 1785–1940* (Ramat Gan, 1999), p. xviii.
15 Ibid., p. 84.
16 Velma Bourgeois Richmond, *Chivalric Stories as Children's Literature: Edwardian Retellings in Words and Pictures* (Jefferson, NC, 2014).
17 Siberry, *New Crusaders*, p. 149.
18 Megan L. Morris, 'Introduction: Victorian Crusades Literature', *The Crusades Project,* University of Rochester, US, <http://d.lib.rochester.edu/crusades/text/nineteenth-century-literature-introduction>, [accessed 10 May 2016].
19 Vaninskaya, 'English Literature', pp. 279–80.
20 Girouard, *Return to Camelot*, pp. 27–38; Siberry, *New Crusaders*, pp. 112–22. For Scott's European influence, see M. Pittock, ed., *The Reception of Walter Scott in Europe* (London, 2006).
21 Walter Scott, *The Talisman*, vol. III, Tales of the Crusaders (Edinburgh, 1825).
22 Walter Scott, *The Talisman*, vol. XXXVIII, The Waverley Novels (Edinburgh, 1860), p. 5.
23 James Watt, 'Orientalism and Empire', in *The Cambridge Companion to Fiction in the Romantic Period*, eds. Richard Maxwell and Katie Trumpener (Cambridge, 2008), pp. 138–39.

24 Scott, *The Talisman* (1860), pp. 35–36; Lincoln, *Walter Scott and Modernity*, p. 111.
25 Megan L. Morris, 'Sir Walter Scott's The Betrothed (1825) and The Talisman (1825)', *The Crusades Project*, University of Rochester, US, <http://d. lib.rochester.edu/camelot/text/sir-walter-scott-betrothed-talisman>, [accessed 14 May 2014]; Scott, *The Talisman*, 1860, p. 501.
26 Morris, 'Scott's The Betrothed and The Talisman'.
27 Ibid.
28 Walter Scott, 'Chivalry', 1815, *Encyclopædia Britannica* (Britannica.com, 2015), <www.britannica.com/topic/Sir-Walter-Scott-on-chivalry-1987278>, [accessed 3 July 2015].
29 Quoted in Roderick Cavaliero, *Ottomania: The Romantics and the Myth of the Islamic Orient* (London, 2010), p. 170.
30 Morris, 'Introduction'.
31 Joseph Bristow, *Empire Boys: Adventures in a Man's World* (London, 1991), p. 58; Jeffrey Richards, 'Popular Imperialism and the Image of the Army in Juvenile Literature', in *Popular Imperialism and the Military, 1850–1950*, ed. John M. MacKenzie (Manchester, 1992), p. 87.
32 Vaninskaya, 'English Literature', p. 280; Siberry, *New Crusaders*, p. 158.
33 Gavin Budge, *Charlotte M. Yonge: Religion, Feminism and Realism in the Victorian Novel* (Bern, 2007), p. 9.
34 Rosemary Mitchell, *Picturing the Past: English History in Text and Image, 1830–1870* (Oxford, 2000), p. 248; Susan Walton, 'Charlotte M. Yonge and the "Historic Harem" of Edward Augustus Freeman', *Journal of Victorian Culture* 11 (2006), p. 247; Suzanne Rahn, 'An Evolving Past: The Story of Historical Fiction and Nonfiction for Children', *The Lion and the Unicorn* 15 (June 1991), p. 4.
35 Elisabeth Jay, 'Yonge, Charlotte Mary (1823–1901)', *ODNB* (Oxford, 2004), <www.oxforddnb.com/view/article/37065>, [accessed 5 March 2014]; Susan Walton, *Imagining Soldiers and Fathers in the Mid-Victorian Era: Charlotte Yonge's Models of Manliness* (Farnham, 2010), p. 4.
36 Charlotte M. Yonge, *The Prince and the Page: A Story of the Last Crusade* (London, 1866), p. 120.
37 Ibid., p. 163.
38 Ibid., p. 23.
39 Ibid., p. vi.
40 See Rosemary Mitchell, 'Healing the Wounds of War: (A)mending the National Narrative in the Historical Publications of Charlotte M. Yonge', *Women's History Review* 20 (2011), p. 800. Edward was 'a graceful and courtly knight, peculiarly gentle in manner, loving music, romances, and all chivalrous accomplishments; [...] gracious to all' (p. 24); a stern commander (p. 104); 'ever just' (p. 116); 'with a sense of the value of definite evidence far in advance of the time, and befitting the English Justinian' (p. 138); 'abstemious' and 'disciplined' (p. 191); 'a greater and better man [...] than England knows or needs.' (p. 256); all Yonge, *The Prince and the Page*.
41 Yonge, *The Prince and the Page*, pp. 202–206.
42 Mitchell, 'Healing the Wounds of War', p. 800.
43 Megan L. Morris, 'Charlotte Mary Yonge's The Prince and the Page: A Story of the Last Crusade', *The Crusades Project*, University of Rochester,

US, <http://d.lib.rochester.edu/crusades/text/prince-and-the-page>, [accessed 14 May 2014].

44 Charlotte M. Yonge, 'Preface', in *Kings of England: A History for Young Children*, 1848, <http://community.dur.ac.uk/c.e.schultze/works/kings_of_england.html>, [accessed 2 May 2014].

45 Richards, 'Image of the Army', p. 87.

46 George A. Henty, *Winning His Spurs: A Tale of the Crusade, Aka The Boy Knight* (London, 1882), p. 54.

47 Peter Newbolt, 'Henty, George Alfred (1832–1902)', *ODNB* (Oxford, 2006), <www.oxforddnb.com/view/article/33827>, [accessed 20 February 2014].

48 Ibid.; Dennis Butts, 'Exploiting a Formula: The Adventure Stories of G.A. Henty (1832–1902)', in *Popular Children's Literature in Britain*, eds. Julia Briggs, Dennis Butts, and Matthew O. Grenby (Aldershot, 2008), pp. 161–62; Sandra Kemp, Charlotte Mitchell, and David Trotter, eds., 'Henty, G. A. [George Alfred Henty]', *The Oxford Companion to Edwardian Fiction* (Oxford, 2005).

49 Henty in his preface to *With Lee in Virginia* (1889), p. 2, quoted in Jerome de Groot, *The Historical Novel* (London, 2009), p. 89.

50 Dennis Butts, '"Tis A Hundred Years Since: G. A. Henty"s With Clive in India and Philip Pullman's The Tin Princess', in *The Presence of the Past in Children's Literature*, ed. Ann Lawson Lucas (Westport, CT, 2003), p. 82.

51 Kemp, Mitchell, and Trotter, 'Henty'.

52 Newbolt, 'Henty'. Henty wrote *The Sovereign Reader* which had multiple editions between 1887 and 1900; see Anna Vaninskaya, '"It Was a Silly System": Writers and Schools, 1870–1939', *The Modern Language Review* 105 (2010), pp. 965–66; Vaninskaya, 'English Literature', p. 280.

53 Paris, *Over the Top*, p. xv.

54 Ibid., pp. xiv–xv.

55 de Groot, *The Historical Novel*, pp. 88–89; Edmund Downey quoted in Butts, 'Henty', p. 152. For Henty as an imperialist see Rahn, 'An Evolving Past', p. 8.

56 Henty, *Winning His Spurs*, pp. 166–74.

57 There is more than a little imperial-orientalist curiosity at work in the novel; for example, Cuthbert, captured by the Saracens, is taken to Jerusalem and later interviewed by the ladies of the governor's harem; see ibid., pp. 144–56.

58 See ibid., pp. 13–27, 88–106, 263–71 and 286.

59 Ibid., p. 235.

60 Ibid., p. 44. See Scott, *Ivanhoe*.

61 Robert Irwin, 'Saladin and the Third Crusade: A Case Study in Historiography and the Historical Novel', in *Companion to Historiography*, ed. Michael Bentley (London, 1997), p. 143.

62 Henty, *Winning His Spurs*, p. 38.

63 Ibid., pp. 52–53.

64 Ibid., pp. 54–55.

65 Quoted from Newbolt's dedication in his novel *The Old Country*; see Sandra Kemp, Charlotte Mitchell, and David Trotter, eds., 'Old Country, The: A Romance', *The Oxford Companion to Edwardian Fiction* (Oxford, 2005).

66 Paris, *Over the Top*, p. xix.
67 Girouard, *Return to Camelot*, p. 283; David Gervais, 'Newbolt, Sir Henry John (1862–1938)', *ODNB* (Oxford, May 2009), <www.oxforddnb.com/view/article/35212>, [accessed 5 March 2014]. Newbolt referred to the line as the 'Frankenstein's Monster that I created.'
68 Paris, *Over the Top*, p. 8; Michael Bright, 'Remembering Sir Henry Newbolt: An Essay and Bibliography', *English Literature in Transition, 1880–1920* 33 (1990), pp. 161–62.
69 Henry Newbolt, *The Book of the Happy Warrior* (London, 1917).
70 Ibid., pp. vii and 275.
71 Vaninskaya, 'English Literature', pp. 276–77.
72 Richmond, *Chivalric Stories*, p. 174.
73 Newbolt, *The Book of the Happy Warrior*, pp. 19 and 48.
74 Ibid., p. 50.
75 Ibid., p. 74.
76 Ibid., pp. 248–53.
77 Henry Newbolt, *The Old Country: A Romance* (London, 1906).
78 Newbolt, *The Book of the Happy Warrior*, p. 170.
79 Ibid., p. 145.
80 Bright, 'Newbolt', p. 160.
81 Newbolt, *Old Country*, p. x.
82 Newbolt, *The Book of the Happy Warrior*, p. 257.
83 Henry Newbolt, *Tales of the Great War* (London, 1916), pp. 248–49.

Bibliography

Primary

Cottin, Sophie. *Matilda and Malek Adhel, the Saracen*. London: R. Dutton, 1809.

Henty, George A. *Winning His Spurs: A Tale of the Crusade, Aka The Boy Knight*. London: Sampson Low, Marston, Searle, & Rivington, 1882.

Hofland, Barbara. *Theodore, or The Crusaders: A Tale for Youth*. London: John Harris, 1921.

Newbolt, Henry. *Tales of the Great War*. London: Longmans Green, 1916.

———. *The Book of the Happy Warrior*. London: Longmans, Green and Co., 1917.

———. *The Old Country: A Romance*. London: Smith, Elder, 1906.

Scott, Walter. 'Chivalry'. *Encyclopædia Britannica*. Britannica.com, 2015. www.britannica.com/topic/Sir-Walter-Scott-on-chivalry-1987278. [Accessed 3 July 2015].

———. *The Talisman*. Vol. III. Tales of the Crusaders. Edinburgh: Archibald Constable and Company, 1825.

———. *The Talisman*. Vol. XXXVIII. The Waverley Novels. Edinburgh: Adam and Charles Black, 1860.

Stanhope, Louisa Sidney. *The Crusaders: An Historical Romance of the Twelfth Century*. London: A.K. Newman, 1820.

Yonge, Charlotte M. 'Preface'. In Kings of England: A History for Young Children, 1848. http://community.dur.ac.uk/c.e.schultze/works/kings_of_england.html. [Accessed 2 May 2014].

———. *The Prince and the Page: A Story of the Last Crusade*. London: Macmillan and Co., 1866.

Secondary

Bratton, Jacqueline S. 'Of England, Home and Duty: The Image of England in Victorian and Edwardian Juvenile Fiction'. In *Imperialism and Popular Culture*. ed. John M. MacKenzie. Manchester: MUP, 1986. pp. 73–93.

Bright, Michael. 'Remembering Sir Henry Newbolt: An Essay and Bibliography'. *English Literature in Transition, 1880–1920* 33 (1990), pp. 155–78.

Bristow, Joseph. *Empire Boys: Adventures in a Man's World*. London: Harper-Collins Academic, 1991.

Budge, Gavin. *Charlotte M. Yonge: Religion, Feminism and Realism in the Victorian Novel*. Bern: Peter Lang, 2007.

Butts, Dennis. 'Exploiting a Formula: The Adventure Stories of G.A. Henty (1832–1902)'. In *Popular Children's Literature in Britain*. eds. Julia Briggs, Dennis Butts, and Matthew O. Grenby. Aldershot: Ashgate, 2008. pp. 149–63.

———. '"Tis A Hundred Years Since: G. A. Henty"s With Clive in India and Philip Pullman's The Tin Princess'. In *The Presence of the Past in Children's Literature*. ed. Ann Lawson Lucas. Westport, CT: Praeger, 2003. pp. 81–87.

Cavaliero, Roderick. *Ottomania: The Romantics and the Myth of the Islamic Orient*. London: I.B. Tauris, 2010.

Gervais, David. 'Newbolt, Sir Henry John (1862–1938)'. *ODNB*. Oxford: OUP, May 2009. www.oxforddnb.com/view/article/35212. [Accessed 5 March 2014].

Girouard, Mark. *Return to Camelot*. London: Yale University Press, 1981.

Groot, Jerome de. *The Historical Novel*. London: Routledge, 2009.

Hinz, Felix. *Kreuzzüge des Mittelalters und der Neuzeit*. Hildesheim: Georg Olms Verlag, 2015.

Irwin, Robert. 'Saladin and the Third Crusade: A Case Study in Historiography and the Historical Novel'. In *Companion to Historiography*. ed. Michael Bentley. London: Taylor and Francis, 1997. pp. 139–52.

Jay, Elisabeth. 'Yonge, Charlotte Mary (1823–1901)'. *ODNB*. Oxford: OUP, 2004. www.oxforddnb.com/view/article/37065. [Accessed 5 March 2014].

Kemp, Sandra, Charlotte Mitchell, and David Trotter. eds. 'Henty, G. A. [George Alfred Henty]'. *The Oxford Companion to Edwardian Fiction*. Oxford: OUP, 2005.

———. eds. 'Old Country, The: A Romance'. *The Oxford Companion to Edwardian Fiction*. Oxford: OUP, 2005.

Lincoln, Andrew. *Walter Scott and Modernity*. Edinburgh: Edinburgh University Press, 2007.

MacKenzie, John M. *Propaganda and Empire: The Manipulation of British Public Opinion 1880–1960*. Manchester: MUP, 1990.

Mangan, James A. 'Noble Specimens of Manhood: Schoolboy Literature and the Creation of a Colonial Chivalric Code'. *The International Journal of the History of Sport* 27 (2010), pp. 389–408.

Mitchell, Rosemary. 'Healing the Wounds of War: (A)mending the National Narrative in the Historical Publications of Charlotte M. Yonge'. *Women's History Review* 20 (2011), pp. 785–808.

———. *Picturing the Past: English History in Text and Image, 1830–1870.* Oxford: OUP, 2000.

Morris, Megan L. 'Charlotte Mary Yonge's The Prince and the Page: A Story of the Last Crusade'. *The Crusades Project*, University of Rochester, US. http://d.lib.rochester.edu/crusades/text/prince-and-the-page. [Accessed 14 May 2014].

———. 'Introduction: Victorian Crusades Literature'. *The Crusades Project*, University of Rochester, US. http://d.lib.rochester.edu/crusades/text/nineteenth-century-literature-introduction. [Accessed 10 May 2016].

———. 'Sir Walter Scott's The Betrothed (1825) and The Talisman (1825)'. *The Crusades Project*, University of Rochester, US. http://d.lib.rochester.edu/camelot/text/sir-walter-scott-betrothed-talisman. [Accessed 14 May 2014].

Newbolt, Peter. 'Henty, George Alfred (1832–1902)'. *ODNB*. Oxford: OUP, 2006. www.oxforddnb.com/view/article/33827. [Accessed 20 February 2014].

Paris, Michael. *Over the Top: The Great War and Juvenile Literature in Britain.* London: Praeger, 2004.

———. *Warrior Nation.* London: Reaktion Books, 2000.

Pittock, Murray, ed. *The Reception of Walter Scott in Europe.* London: Bloomsbury, 2006.

Rahn, Suzanne. 'An Evolving Past: The Story of Historical Fiction and Non-fiction for Children'. *The Lion and the Unicorn* 15 (June 1991), pp. 1–26.

Richards, Jeffrey. 'Popular Imperialism and the Image of the Army in Juvenile Literature'. In *Popular Imperialism and the Military, 1850–1950.* ed. John M. MacKenzie. Manchester: MUP, 1992. pp. 80–108.

Richmond, Velma Bourgeois. *Chivalric Stories as Children's Literature: Edwardian Retellings in Words and Pictures.* Jefferson, NC: McFarland & Company, 2014.

Shadur, Joseph. *Young Travelers to Jerusalem: The Holy Land in American and English Juvenile Literature, 1785–1940.* Ramat Gan: Ingeborg Rennert Center for Jerusalem Studies, 1999.

Siberry, Elizabeth. 'Tasso and the Crusades: History of a Legacy'. *Journal of Medieval History* 19 (1993), pp. 163–69.

———. *The New Crusaders: Images of the Crusades in the 19th and Early 20th Centuries.* Aldershot: Ashgate, 2000.

Vaninskaya, Anna. 'English Literature'. *Journal of Victorian Culture* 12 (2007), pp. 276–81.

———. '"It Was a Silly System": Writers and Schools, 1870–1939'. *The Modern Language Review* 105 (2010), pp. 952–75.

Walton, Susan. 'Charlotte M. Yonge and the "Historic Harem" of Edward Augustus Freeman'. *Journal of Victorian Culture* 11 (2006), pp. 226–55.

————. *Imagining Soldiers and Fathers in the Mid-Victorian Era: Charlotte Yonge's Models of Manliness*. Farnham: Ashgate, 2010.

Watt, James. 'Orientalism and Empire'. In *The Cambridge Companion to Fiction in the Romantic Period*. eds. Richard Maxwell and Katie Trumpener, Cambridge: CUP, 2008. pp. 129–42.

3 'May God punish England!'

Pseudo-crusading language and Holy War motifs in postcards of the First World War

Felix Hinz

Crusading has long been understood as a facet of Christian Holy War; one which can attract the full rhetoric and imagery of a divinely inspired and approved conflict.[1] The all-encompassing and emotive nature of warfare and the need to mobilise whole populations in the modern era have exacerbated the tendencies of propagandists to enlist whatever symbols were on hand to best prosecute the war effort. The German deployment of crusading language and Holy War motifs in the First World War demonstrates this appropriation whilst resisting hard distinctions between perceptions of the war as a Holy War *or* a crusade. Rather, as this chapter shows, crusading was closely intertwined in the presentation of the war as holy.

Postcards as a medium during the First World War

Postcards are a neglected historical source. One reason is that there are no official archives collecting them systematically. To date, only a small number of databases for deltiology exist; these are mainly focussed on postcards which have never been sent to anyone, and none of them can claim completeness.[2] The most extensive and well-ordered collections are still owned by private persons, most notably in Germany the collector and historian Otto May, from whom most of the postcards presented here derive.[3]

Until the beginning of the twentieth century, postcards were a specifically German domain,[4] meaning that half of the German picture postcards of the time were exported. They were known as letters for the 'humble man' (in contrast to the more familiar letters written by people from the educated classes) because they did not necessarily need a formal structure, well-phrased sentences or even meaningful content. Due to the limited amount of space for written messages on a postcard, it was convenient to express oneself in an abbreviated cable style or by using slogans or catchphrases. Moreover, spare time was very rare, especially for members of the working classes, hence there was simply not enough free time to write conventional letters. After the Prussian postal service had overcome its concerns about the secrecy of letters in 1870, the postcard began its rise. This was in part because postcards could be purchased for a few pennies, and sending a postcard was only half as expensive as sending a letter. Additionally, it should be noted that in the days when only very few families owned a telephone, written communication was used differently and more frequently than today. Even in rural areas postmen delivered letters and postcards several times a day – in the big cities up to eight times. Therefore, it was common to arrange a meeting or to announce an appearance on the same day via postcards.

Soon the back of a postcard, which was originally a blank space intended for written messages, was completely covered with pictures, often with photos of prominent places. Because not everyone could afford to take their own photographs, postcards at that time fulfilled needs which are today covered by smartphones. In order to further fuel the rapidly growing postcard industry the producers soon came up with the idea to start producing series of postcards and corresponding scrapbooks. This became enormously successful and a new 'mass craze'[5] in the form of a collecting mania spread rapidly all over Western Europe, the US and the British Empire. With regard to art postcards it also included the upper classes; even Queen Victoria started to accumulate postcards.[6] The collections were presented in frames displayed on walls or simply gathered in scrapbooks which then were presented to visitors in order to exchange cards and thereby complete the collection. Favourite motifs were skylines of towns, picture stories, beautiful women, children, animals, means of transport and uniforms of the army.[7] The postcard industry also entered the field of politics by producing and printing caricatures. For this very reason postcards were soon utilised as a medium for propaganda. The government of Kaiser Wilhelm II recognised instantly how much influence one could have on public opinion by presenting certain political and historical narratives. As a consequence, postcards with patriotic motifs were spread, which found their way into the homes of the lower classes who could thereby stress their patriotism.

During the First World War more than twenty-eight billion postal mailings were sent by the German Army alone, of which approximately 25% were postcards.[8] Because the army's postal service was free of charge and the German postcard industry, whose interests were represented by a special organisation,[9] needed compensation for its loss of exports, the number of propaganda postcards vastly exceeded the number of postcards produced before the war.[10]

The impact of these postcards on public opinion, however, is difficult to estimate. In order to provide a solid basis for analysis concerning the usage of terms, I want to set out the constituent components. According to Anett Holzheid, the postcard can generally be described as a communicative entity consisting of five possible single elements:

1   Carrier material (usually card)
2   Sender's message, consisting of the recipient's address, a text message and optionally the sender's address
3   Picture elements produced by the sender
4   Carrier message (formal print of the postal service – textual applications printed on the carrier by the industry; for instance, legends, slogans, prayers, verses)
5   Picture elements on the carrier (industrial picture applications as well as further quotations taken from the area of symbolic culture; for instance, from songs or hymns)[11]

In the context of this chapter, the explicit focus can only be on the fourth and fifth elements. Moreover, it seems inappropriate to rely on analytical methods taken from the field of art history because the meaning of a picture postcard should not be derived from a broad interpretation but rather what was intended to be grasped at first sight. While the publishing house can often be identified, the size of the print runs are usually unknown. Data about how often the postcards were bought and sent and whether the senders referred to the picture within their messages – and if yes, how – would be even more useful. When the postcards were sent to someone, it seems logical that the political messages included in the imagery were also in line with the interests of the sender, otherwise he or she would have chosen a different motif. Nevertheless, the question still remains: can postcards be taken as reliable sources for research about mentality or affiliation, or instead as indicative of the publisher's ideological position? An analysis of the relation of individual communications and mass-produced pictures would be fruitfully employed with regard to enquiries in the fields of historical culture and the history of media.

To be able to interpret picture postcards from the First World War the following background has to be considered. While the Entente

Powers established national propaganda offices very early in the conflict to coordinate the design of the picture postcards, mostly showing a ruthless demonization of the wartime enemies, the German market was initially determined by supply and demand.[12] The gradually emerging control stations, peaking at about fifty, saw their main task as restraining politically unwanted motifs, especially those that denounced the opponent in a particularly vulgar way.[13] By 1914 about 500 postcard images had been declared as repulsive and had been forbidden by the German side.[14] This implies that on the part of the Central Powers early on, a certain perspective was communicated which evoked impressions of honour and dignity in a war that soon turned ugly.

The compulsory component in this context was religion. Besides the known power of the idea of Holy War[15] to mobilise the troops, there was, for Germany, another aspect, namely the 'Kulturkampf'; German policies designed to reduce the political power of the Roman Catholic Church. For the first time in German history a Protestant dynasty, the House of Hohenzollern, occupied the imperial throne. Consequently, the Reich had a high value, especially for the German Protestants. Ernst Tröltsch, one of the leading representatives of the so-called cultural Protestantism, emphasised this in a speech from August 1914:

> Since we have an emperor and an empire, our motto tends to be: With God for Kaiser and Reich! Well then today each of those three words which it contains weighs a thousand-fold [...]. In this hour we also pray with each prayer the deep and serious fiery and strong vow: With God for Kaiser and Reich! May God help us keep it![16]

Bismarck made sure that in the state established in 1871 Protestants occupied almost all positions of power. Thereby the Catholics – still more than a third of the population – were threatened with becoming second-class citizens.[17] The French in particular took advantage of this fact and accused their Catholic co-religionists in Germany of betraying Rome during war, thus trying to split up the Reichswehr. The war, they alleged, was actually a war against Rome by the Protestants.[18] German Catholics indignantly rejected this accusation and hoped (just as the German Jews) to profit politically from their loyalty to emperor and Reich. Wilhelm II for his part, despite all inner disputes, proclaimed that he no longer knew different parties or confessions but only Germans.

The opinion that God and the Reich were connected was deeply rooted in German society, going back to the traditions of the Holy Roman Empire. Like many other nations of the nineteenth century the Germans claimed to be the new 'chosen nation.' When the establishment of a German state was finally, and painstakingly, achieved in 1871, it seemed indeed to be a divine wonder. 'Gott mit uns!' – 'God [is] with us!' – was the war cry of the German armies, which was first heard against Napoleon I and then again against Napoleon III, and it seemed to have been proven accurate. Therefore, the new empire bristled with moral and military self-confidence. 'We Germans fear God, but nothing else in the World', boasted Bismarck in 1888.[19] Other nations also considered themselves as especially close to God and interpreted the war right from the beginning as a Holy War.[20]

France in the nineteenth and early twentieth centuries, for example, often regarded itself as the eldest daughter of the Roman Church. The German culture was displayed by the French as atheistic, raw and barbaric, while France fought for the 'Catholic principle'; its victory was a triumph of the Catholic and Christian idea. The literal announcement was 'Fighting against France is fighting against God.'[21] Germany on the other hand was the shelter of the absolute evil.[22] And of course God was also on the side of England and even more of the US, 'God's own country', who uninhibitedly publicised their wars as crusades, shown most markedly in the government propaganda posters and films 'Pershing's Crusaders'.[23]

'God with us!' – the German battle as a Holy War

The question about the relationship between Christianity and violence is as old as Christianity itself. Indisputable was that God showed mercy for all sinners and therefore for Christian soldiers as well – a group who were particularly sinful. Wilhelm II demanded a loyal attitude towards religion even from troops of the German Army whose Supreme Commander he was. On the occasion of the administration of an oath in 1909 the Kaiser said the following:

> The one of my soldiers who has a low opinion of religion and God is no good. He will lose his honour, and is not dignified to wear my uniform! [...] Only he who can rely firmly on his God can be a proper soldier.[24]

Captain Baerensprung had already expressed his thoughts about the education of infantrymen in such a way in 1907:

There has to be a firm belief in God's leadership and almighti-
ness, which inspires the soldier who himself, I want to say, comes
close to the fatalism of the Mohammedan which leads him like the
Mohammedan with a defiance of death into the battle. The fear of
death is in human nature. A good soldier has to and will overcome
it in the belief of the almighty God [...] who rewards a loyal performance of duty, up to the ultimate sacrifice of one's own life, in
the afterlife.[25]

In Bussler's speech, *Patriotism from the Pulpit*, it was additionally said:

The duty of clerks to foster a patriotic spirit by preaching sermons
is even intensified by the circumstances of our time; because the
spirit of revolution, lawlessness and unpatriotic attitudes is best
fought by the Christian fear of God.[26]

Protestant clerks were seen as perfect mediators for patriotism (for instance, Luther was presented as a German hero who freed his country
from the 'Servitude of Rome'). During the reign of Wilhelm II, being
a good German was equated to being a good Protestant. The spheres
of patriotism and religion were therefore consistently intermingled,
for instance when national ceremonies were specifically celebrated by
going to church, singing chorales, patriotic hymns, and delivering sermons and speeches. Very similar to this was a report written down by
a girl in her diary at the beginning of the First World War:

2nd September 1914, Sedan Day![27] Again there was no school. We
gathered at the schoolyard at nine o'clock to move in well-ordered
lines into the church, where there was a mass said to celebrate the
day. [...] At the corner of every fourth bench sat a teacher to make
sure that no nuisance was caused.
    Then the pastor delivered a speech. He commemorated the
Battle of Sedan in the year 1871 and compared it to the Battle
of Tannenberg by saying that it was even bigger than the Battle
of Sedan, that there had been more captives and dead men. God
was standing behind our brave soldiers and praised their weap-
ons. Uncountable Russian [soldiers] had died in the battle around
the Masuric swamps. The Lord beat them with men, and horse
and wagon, he shouted down from the pulpit. After that the organ
started in and we sung, 'Great God we praise you'. Then everyone
donated two pennies into the collection box. This time the amount
is designated for widows and orphans of the warriors. [...] Then we
went home. [...].

2nd September 1915 [...]. Actually we would have to go to church again in order to celebrate the old victory of 1870/1871 but in between we have celebrated so many new victories that the Sedan day was turned into a memorial day for the Reformation.[28]

It can be recognised that the writer does not realise the blend between religion and patriotism any more. Here the patriotic education was taken over by the Protestant priest.

At the beginning of the First World War a noticeably large number of German soldiers attended military church services seeking atonement. This aspect of religion accompanied every war conducted by Christians. Yet God in his role as guardian and comforter is not our topic. We are interested here in the Christian God as a God of war, which Pope Gregory VII had especially promoted and made acceptable for the Latin World.[29] In the context of this chapter, therefore, we are looking for the militant God of the crusades, the trigger-happy Son of God who leads the heavenly armies against Gog and Magog. And, in contrast to an opinion recently presented by Christine Brooks,[30] we can discover these motifs on a German postcard from 1915 (Figure 3.1). Here Christ fulfils the dual function of protecting the soldiers, yet on the other hand pointing at the enemy; importantly he stands next to them and not protectively in front of them. The German commanding officer appears to look Jesus in the eye while giving the order to shoot

Figure 3.1 'In the trench – lo, I am with you always. (Mat 28:20)', Germany, 1915.

and from the way Jesus looks back at him it seems like he agrees. This shows that the German shots are in his interest and sanctified as serving a good and just cause – *Deus lo vult*.

A set of images that depicted the Constantine legend at the Battle of the Milvian Bridge (312 AD) were also aggressively promoted. According to Eusebius of Caesarea, Constantine saw a sign in the sky before the battle and the words 'by this sign you will conquer'. Having put the symbol of the cross on the shields of his soldiers, he was victorious and became Roman Emperor. In retrospect, 312 AD was seen as the point from which Christianity was slowly and officially established in the Roman Empire. On the other hand, the usage of the cross as a military sign hints at a shallow understanding of a formerly pacifistic Christian faith. This utterly pagan motive once more points out the assumption of a close relation between religion and nation – and the Germans claimed to follow the direct succession of Rome, both religious and imperial (Figure 3.2).

Figure 3.2 'By this sign we will conquer!', Germany, 1915.

The German postcard shows, similar to the one described by Eusebius, a shining cross above the sun. An infantryman piously takes off his helmet and goes on his knees for a prayer while a dragoon admires the wonder in silence. Between the soldier and a building runs a river, which might lead to the conclusion that there is a bridge in close proximity to the place where the German troops, to whom this sign is dedicated, will win the battle – and the war.

Several aspects were also tied to the religious tradition of the German campaigns of 1813 against Napoleon. This primarily applied to the symbol of the Iron Cross, which the Prussian King Frederick William III donated in 1813. His purpose for this bravery medal, based on the Napoleonic Cross of the *Legion d'honneur* and intentionally connected to the Black Cross of the Teutonic Knights, was to establish an idealistic order that could be joined by anybody who especially deserved it fighting for the patriotic – and therefore holy – cause. Class distinctions or ranks did not matter in this case. Hence the carriers of this cross were effectively brothers-in-arms in a Holy War. The Iron Cross was re-established during the Unification War in 1870 and proved very popular. During the First World War, more than five million of them were awarded to the approximately thirteen million German soldiers (Figure 3.3).[31]

A very appealing postcard picture from 1916 establishes a relation between four crosses; that is, the Iron Cross, the Red Cross, a burial cross and the crucifix. Firstly, as the most important, the Iron Cross is mentioned, accompanied by the Red Cross which was very present in the military.[32] While the upper part depicts life on earth, the burial cross refers to the omnipresence of death for soldiers and the crucifix refers to an afterlife, which was also closely linked to life on earth in the way that the Iron Cross and the crucifix would represent somehow the nuts and bolts of German warfare. Wounds as well as death were explained in this picture as being a sacrifice for God (crucifix) and fatherland (Iron Cross) and were thereby filled with a meaning of legitimation.

Leaving the crucifix aside, there was at that time a tradition of 'the three crosses'. In 1915 the former director of the theatre in Frankfurt, Carl Specht, composed a song for soldiers. 'The Three Crosses' was written for a singer accompanied by the piano, and printed leaflets for it still exist.[33] Another popular motif was the combination of fierce biblical quotations and visual depictions of crusaders, which indirectly interpreted the war as a crusade. Printed next to this type of motif, which was already well known before the war, were verses from the Bible which were often complemented by artists or publishers.

Figure 3.3 'Iron Cross. In heroic legends your fame is great. After battle the wounds heal where the Red Cross-flag greets. / You, to whom a Cross indicates the honour of a hero, you country, whose dead are resting under a cross, you country, which bows at any cross: By this sign you will conquer! / You dead heroes, your graves are marked with crosses without name. You at the cross, the proud of any Christian, Lord, help us gain victory! Amen. By this sign we will conquer!', Germany, 1916.

58   *Felix Hinz*

Figure 3.4 'With God we shall do valiantly.' (Ps 60:12), Germany, 1916.

These supplements usually contained patriotic and motivating content, as well as interpreting Christian life as a battle; they thus turned a potential or real battle into service to God. In accordance with that purpose the following lines were written on a German postcard from 1905: 'Be thou faithful unto death, and I will give thee a crown of life.' (Rev. 2:10). On a postcard from the year 1912 another aphorism can be found: 'God is our refuge and strength.' (Ps. 46:1) and 'A Christian should always be visible wherever he stands – confidently and without fear.' – Germany, stamped 1912 (Figure 3.4).

Moreover, the occurrence of German war symbols on postcards from the World Wars was not a rare phenomenon, as one can find, for instance, the Reich's battle flag on the card printed above. It is obvious that the characters are usually not presented as knights of the Teutonic Order but rather as either crusaders in general or as representatives of the Order of Saint John (also known as the Knights Hospitaller). Additionally, it has to be mentioned that the Bailiwick of Brandenburg is the German Protestant branch of the Knights Hospitaller.[34] Members of this Order belonged to the Prussian high society, such as Otto von Bismarck. The heads of the Order, the so-called Herrenmeister, were Prussian Princes, including the son of the Kaiser, Eitel Friedrich (r.1907–26).[35] Regardless, there is no lack of postcards with motifs which refer to the Teutonic Order. However, these usually contain an obvious reference to the Baltic region and a general relationship to Holy War, which is not directly considered in the postcards dealt with in this chapter.

The patriotic militant tradition was continued even after the war by the Young German Order (Jungdeutscher Orden), which also incorporated symbols closely related to the Order of Saint John. The Young German Order, of which numerous postcards still exist, had grown to at least 300,000 members before it was banned by the National Socialists in the process of *Gleichschaltung* in 1933.[36] Furthermore, there are several prayers to be found on postcards, which – despite trivialising pictorial motives – not only ask for a happy homecoming of fathers and brothers but specifically for the victory of German arms. Even the Lord's Prayer was reinterpreted in a military sense, as if the German Army – blessed by Christ himself – fought on earth to constitute the Kingdom of Heaven (Figure 3.5).

Patriotic supplements were often added to the Our Father prayer; for instance, 'As we forgive those who trespass against us, we simply fight for our countries' houses which they furnish with fire and murder.'[37] Besides this there were pseudo-prayers, which again dated back to the time of the German campaign of 1813. Perhaps the most popular postcard topic

Figure 3.5 'For thine is the kingdom [Reich!], the power, and the glory, for ever and ever. Amen!', Germany, 1914.

VATER, ICH PREISE DICH!
'S IST JA KEIN KAMPF FÜR DIE GÜTER DER ERDE;
DAS HEILIGSTE SCHÜTZEN WIR MIT DEM SCHWERTE;
DRUM, FALLEND UND SIEGEND, PREIS' ICH DICH,
GOTT, DIR ERGEB' ICH MICH!
THEODOR KÖRNER

Figure 3.6 'FATHER, I praise Thee! / Not for the goods of this earth we are fighting: / To guard the holiest, our swords are smiting. / Falling in triumph, I praise Thee. / My God, I trust Thee!', Germany, 1914.

was represented by the *Prayer at Battle* by Theodor Körner (1791–1813). Körner was a German poet who joined the Lützow Free Corps in the battle against Napoleonic rule. He also wrote patriotic poems during the war, verses which were loved by his fellow countrymen and strengthened their fighting spirit. When he died in battle he was stylised as a German national hero. Körner penned the *Prayer at Battle*, which in its most meaningful passages is to be found on countless German postcards either using pictures of the campaign of 1813 or directly connecting the text to pictures of the First World War. This prayer was a war prayer that declared the battle of the Germans as a holy cause so that here the crusading spirit can clearly be recognised (Figure 3.6).

The poet on this card is depicted in a heroic view from below, while his hands are clutched around the handle of the sword as if he was praying. Incidentally, the shape of the handle is the shape of a cross. While his eyes are directed towards the sky, his face is made to appear paler and therefore more Germanic by brightening up his black hair and by broadening his face in order to present him as a true German hero. His love and loyalty, as well as his willingness to sacrifice his life for the 'holy cause' is even more emphasised by highlighting his engagement ring.[38] Lines from another poet of the same campaign – Ernst Moritz Arndt – can be placed in a similar category. His pithy aphorism 'The God who made iron grow did not want slaves!' would find many uses in the Second World War.

The fact that the hostilities were started by Austria-Hungary and Germany, who then invaded the neutral Belgium, immediately raised the question of war guilt. A picture postcard explicitly approved in 1915 by the German Supreme Army Command and the Austrian Press Ministry specifically allocated guilt to the statesmen of the Entente. The emperors accusingly point them out on the right of the image, having armed forces at their back, and on the left side the oppressed civilian population of Europe endorse them. This labelled the war as a judgement of God.

The fact that Britain, with its German-influenced royal house, refused a familial alliance and instead affiliated with the Entente led to an angry bitterness from the Hohenzollerns. Wilhelm felt betrayed and deserted by his cousin George V. The Germans became fully aware of

Figure 3.7 'May God punish England! – May He punish it!', Germany, 1914.

Figure 3.8 'May God punish the traitorous Italy and destroy England', Germany, 1915.

the British supremacy at sea, and as a consequence their propaganda evoked the wrath of God. The slogan 'May God punish England!' became a common greeting, to which the addressed person had to reply 'May he punish it!' These martial slogans can also be found on the postcard in Figure 3.6. Down from the cloud-veiled sky, a huge executioner's sword had been thrust at England and became stuck there; the holy meaning is underlined by a shining cross in front of a dark background – a divine warning sign. In the four corners of the card, hourglasses are depicted with their upper parts already empty, which might have the meaning 'England, your time is up.' Additionally, the white cliffs of Dover illustrated the view from the south. To be more precise, they took the perspective from the direction where the German air vessels and planes took off in 1915 or from whence an invasion of the island might have (but never has) been started (Figure 3.7).

Later Italy was cursed as well because it entered the war on the side of the Entente, despite the existing Triple Alliance of 1882. It was therefore repudiated as faithless. These mottos were to be found on numerous picture postcards, occasionally in combination. On at least one postcard an angry God threw thunderbolts out of the crown of a German oak at enemies pictured as satanic dragons, faced like St George by the surrounded Central Powers (Figure 3.8).

The Kaiser – 'messenger of God'?

An especially dynamic aspect of the German postcard propaganda and the counter-propaganda of the Allies focussed on the person of Wilhelm II, the most powerful figure of the Central Powers. The notorious vanity of Wilhelm, who put the greatest value on playing to the gallery, made him the first real media star in history and often caused embarrassment to friend and foe. Exploiting the latest techniques of photography for his cause, the Kaiser went so far as cancelling public appearances at short notice when the weather was not perfect (which is why there is still a German saying, which refers to *Kaiserwetter,* emperor's weather, when the sun is shining).

His pithy appearance and his childish addiction to disguise and bombastic self-expression were both his strength and his weakness – and provided his opponents a perfect target. Approximately 80% of the Entente caricatures on postcards display the Kaiser as the dominant motif during the First World War.[39] The reason why almost no caricatures ridiculing him were drawn in Germany until 1918 was the fact that Wilhelm II punished critical remarks as *lèse-majesté*. Nonetheless, Wilhelm II is the German monarch who appeared most often on caricatures. His peculiar style of beard (the neatly twirled endings of his moustache) meant that he could be recognised quickly, which was very important for caricatures, even when the drawings were distorted. Even before the war, foreign postcards made fun of the Kaiser by illustrating him as a peacock, an allusion to his often-upright posture, or as a standing sausage which almost breaks through its own skin.

Wilhelm did not stop assuring everyone that despite his love for the military, parades and battleships, he was no warmonger. On postcards he called on God as a witness, asserting that he did not want the war but was forced into it. His followers bought into his conviction, but not so his enemies. On numerous postcards he presented himself – following the dictum of Bismarck – as pious and strong. On one postcard he showed 'devotion in the field' – a nod to the 1914 war prayer arranged by him:

> Almighty and merciful God! Lord of Hosts! In humility we ask you to lend thy almighty aid to the German fatherland. Bless the entire German power. Lead us to victory and give us grace that we treat also your enemies as Christians. Let us soon reach lasting peace for the honour and independence of Germany.[40]

Throne and altar in close relation formed an important symbol for the legitimation of his reign. This becomes obvious when looking at the church-building programme he initiated soon after he ascended the throne. The most popular church that was built in the context of this program was the Kaiser-Wilhelm-Gedächtniskirche (Kaiser Wilhelm Memorial Church) in Berlin, which is still very well known in Germany. The ultimate peak of the programme was the construction of the Protestant Church of the Redeemer in Jerusalem. Its tower is even higher than the tower of the Church of the Holy Sepulchre and was built on the former ground of the first hospital of the Knights of St John of Jerusalem. The glittering inaugural ceremony was attended by the Kaiser and his wife in person in order to place themselves in a line of tradition with the above-mentioned Constantine. The journey of the Kaiser and his wife to Palestine from 11 October until 26 November 1898 aroused a lot of attention in the media, and not only in Europe.[41]

Again and again Wilhelm demonstrated how he claimed to have received his crown by God's mercy, which appeared pretentious and not contemporary to many people at that time. On the postcard in Figure 3.9, the Kaiser can be seen standing in a commander's posture and looking downhill through his field glasses at a distant scene of war centred upon a burning village. Wilhelm is not only at a great

Figure 3.9 'A man with God at his side always outnumbers his enemies', Germany, 1914.

distance from the soldiers but also from his commanders. Far from the battle, Wilhelm is alone but standing confidently next to the imperial banner. The aphorism 'A man with God at his side always outnumbers his enemies' alludes to the fact that the Central Powers were soon outnumbered and euphemises the point that this thought had been daunting the Kaiser right from the beginning of the war, especially as the formal Supreme Commander of the German troops was not in command himself but had handed the regiments over to Hindenburg and Ludendorff.

On several occasions the Kaiser unhesitatingly continued to represent himself as pious and peaceful. This pose did not fit with the methods of German warfare, which right from the beginning of the war seemed to use all possible means to gain a quick victory and handled the population of Belgium harshly. The Germans first used toxic gas and eventually developed the inhuman plan to force the French army through the so called Bone-crusher of Verdun. Although not all of these were Wilhelm's own ideas, as the formal Supreme Commander of the armed forces he was responsible for these decisions that were neither peaceable, Christian nor knightly.

In 1916, as a partial response to the postcard described before, caricatures which depicted the Kaiser as Nero with a lyre in his hand (instead of the field glasses as on the first postcard) and singing a tune on burning cathedrals were produced in Italy and France. In order to ridicule his pious appearance and his church-building programme, postcards designed in France in 1914 illustrated Wilhelm, very similar to stained glass church windows, as a destroyer of churches rather than as a donor.

The Entente Powers quickly took advantage of this and zeroed in on his person. Especially in the francophone area, which saw the worst of the brutal trench warfare, Wilhelm's religious assurance was bitterly mocked as hypocrisy (Figures 3.11 and 3.12).

Containing an obvious iconographic reference to the famous photograph of the young Kaiser in cuirass and uniform of the *Garde du Corps* (Figure 3.10) and a German postcard on which Wilhelm swears by God that he did not want the war (Figure 3.11), this self-representation is vehemently refuted by a caricature designed by the Swiss Pierre Chatillon (Figure 3.12).[42] According to this caricature, the self-named 'Messenger of God' is rather to be seen as a butcher of human beings.[43] His bright white uniform is contrasted against a blood-stained butcher's apron, and his sabre has turned into a butcher's knife. The Prussian Eagle, whose black feathers indeed seem on the earlier postcard (Figure 3.11) very similar to the feathers of a crow, perches on the helmet, which is typical for the helmet of the *Garde du Corps*. The eagle carries a piece of meat in his beak and is surrounded by a flock of carrion eaters who are served a voluminous meal by the Kaiser. This gives the empty and brutal-looking Kaiser a daunting and soulless expression. He seems to be a puppet of the devil, which ridiculed the printed slogan 'The Messenger of God'.

Even in Germany the religious appearance of the Kaiser was seen as pretentious.[44] This became obvious in the affair of Ludwig Quidde. In 1894 this historian produced a small manuscript about Caligula in which, with regard to the development of a 'megalomania', many people at that time recognised striking parallels to Wilhelm II. Quidde only escaped severe punishment because the Kaiser did not want to start a discussion about potential similarities, which would have been caused by a public trial.[45]

Another French postcard (Figure 3.13) transformed the German saying 'God with us' into bitter irony. It depicted the unholy trinity

Figure 3.10 This photograph of Wilhelm II (1905) was also distributed as a postcard.

Figure 3.11 'In the face of God and history I am of pure conscience: I did not want this war', Germany, 1914.

Figure 3.12 'The Messenger of God', France 1915.

Figure 3.13 'God with us – Father, Son and Holy Ghost', France, 1915.

consisting of Crown Prince Wilhelm, presented as a rabbit playing with military toys; the Kaiser, surrounded by a halo and holding a Red Cross card; and the Prussian Eagle, which was drawn in the shape of a vulture. Moreover, the background was very similar to a sacral building, and the three were depicted in niches, like statues of saints. The angels flanking the inscription 'Gott mit uns' could hardly hold back laughter with regard to this sanctimonious trinity.[46]

A French card (Figure 3.14) showed the emperor – in a devilish reinterpretation of the German war cry 'God is with us' – as the Antichrist. In this image, God was with the Kaiser, but in a very different way than *he* claimed. Here Christ was seen, suffering another martyrdom, tied to the emperor's horse's tail and dragged to death over Europe's battlefields. The Kaiser cracked a whip which illustrated him as a scourge of God and a divine plague. With the exception of one naked tree, the clouds of smoke and the many burial crosses let the world appear as a desert of death to underline how effective Wilhelm's destruction had already been (Figure 3.14).

Although this is a French postcard, the slogan is written in German and English which can be taken as a hint that the message was not only addressed to the French but also to the British and Americans, and maybe even to Germans – especially those who were living in Alsace-Lorraine.

The Kaiser liked to see himself in the role of a knight of the Order of St John already before the war.[47] Widely known was the picture of Wilhelm in *Punch* magazine, which depicted him as a Teutonic Knight

Figure 3.14 'Gott mit uns – God is with us', France (between 1914 and 1918).

playing with a drawn sword lying on his shoulder, apparently hypocritically speaking to the unarmed Saladin standing in front of him: 'What!! The Christian powers putting pressure upon you, my dear friend!! Horrible! I can't imagine how people can do such things!'[48] The caricature 'Cook's Crusader' from 1898 was also printed on postcards and referred to the journey of the Kaiser to the Orient in the same year. During this tour he honoured Saladin by visiting his grave in Damascus and dedicating a bronze-guilt laurel wreath, with the inscription 'from one great ruler to another,' which caused dismay among Western nations. In 1920 it was removed as a war trophy by T.E. Lawrence (of Arabia) and is today exhibited in the Imperial War Museum in London.[49]

Wilhelm even had himself portrayed as an instrument of God, as an executor of divine justice. On a postcard printed in 1914 (Figure 3.15) he looked sternly at the spectator, wearing no jewellery and a plain shirt decorated with a cross. Only the crown in the upper-left corner hinted at his imperial dignity. He was clasping the sword, which was also a symbol of justice. Here he presented himself as a new Saladin who throws the assumptive into the dust. Therefore Wilhelm, who admired the crusader

Figure 3.15 'The judge of the world', Germany, 1914.

novels of Sir Walter Scott, saw himself not just as a crusader in a Christian sense but as a universal-crusader for the cause of the Abrahamic God.[50]

At this point we need to address the fact that prevented the war from declining into pseudo-crusading language even more than portrayed so far: all larger parties in the conflict had Muslim fighters in their ranks. This applied to the extensive French colonial empire as well as to the even more expansive British Empire. The Central Powers aspired towards taking advantage of this and therefore tried to instigate a revolt (through the calling of a *jihad*) against British rule amongst the Muslim population.[51] It is also important to consider that Britain would not have been in the condition to finance the costs of the war without the immense income of (the partly Muslim) India. After all, the Central Powers had the most powerful Muslim state amongst their lines, the Ottoman Empire, which not only protected the important sanctuaries of Islam but whose sultan also claimed the caliphate. Yet the caliph was able to proclaim the Holy War of the Muslims. So it happened that the same Wilhelm who presented himself as demonstratively Protestant in Europe not only pressured the sultan to enter the war on his side but in 1915 also to officially proclaim *jihad* against the Allies (Figure 3.16).

Figure 3.16 'Help comes from God and victory is near. – The Sultan proclaims Jihad – the great Holy War against England, Russia and France', Germany, 1915.

Figure 3.17 'Be strong and hang on as you have until now. Peace be with you and with your people. And you shall form a firm alliance. Soon will be blessed the covenant – the new!', Germany, 1915.

Of course, this caused difficulties: because of their oppressive policies the Ottomans were not necessarily liked in all parts of the Muslim World. Consequently, the Germans in Flanders now fought their allegedly Holy War in a Christian sense, while in Palestine they literally put themselves under the green flag of the Prophet and even defended Jerusalem for the caliph in 1917 against the British General Allenby.

So, whose God was this, looking at the contemplator from the postcard in Figure 3.17? Here again a new covenant is mentioned – yet on a higher Abrahamic level. It seems less important in this context that any drawings or pictures of God are forbidden in the Islamic world because the motif was only designated for German-speaking areas.[52] It would be interesting to find out how far the Ottoman military postal service used postcards as a medium of communication.

Conclusion

In conclusion, it can be said that the First World War from the German perspective was indeed promoted as a Holy War – in a religious as well as in a secular, national sense – but not explicitly as a Christian crusade[53] because the war was actually a world war that spread across the peoples of the book with Christians, Jews and Muslims against other Christians, Jews and Muslims. Of course, the Entente nations were not willing to accept the German claim to lead a war in favour of God without criticism. Their counter-propaganda was especially aimed at the Kaiser whose conceited posturing offered significant potential for mockery. In Germany the impact of the Holy War propaganda was moderate. Given the years of ongoing horror, which the churches did not tire to justify as religious and moral purification, many Germans and especially soldiers turned away from Church and faith.[54] Soon after the beginning of the war they largely stayed away from the field church services. The German policy in the postcard propaganda to focus on honour and religion was not as successful as anticipated because romantic motifs were preferred by soldiers.[55] Furthermore, the religious propaganda offered several opportunities to the Entente to attack which could not been repaid in an appropriate manner.

With the end of the war in 1918 the postcard mania in Germany also came to a halt.[56] While a significant amount of resources had been invested in the further development of telephones, the charges for the postal service were considerably raised and it was not appropriate to express the depressed atmosphere via the medium of the picture postcard. Despite some market upturns in the 1920s and 1960s it has never again reached the social importance it had between 1900 and 1918.[57]

Notes

1 The broad interpretation of crusading was considered the 'generalist' approach by Giles Constable's historiographical survey; Giles Constable, 'The Historiography of the Crusades', in *The Crusades from the Perspective of Byzantium and the Muslim World*, eds. Angeliki E. Laiou and Roy Parviz Mottahedeh (Washington, DC, 2001), pp. 14–15.
2 There is a collection of 300,000 postcards at the Museum für Kommunikation, Berlin, <http://sammlungen.museumsstiftung.de/ansichtskarten>, [accessed 08 March 2017]. Very useful is the digital version of the collection of S. Giesbrecht, *Historische Bildpostkarten*, University of Osnabrück <www.bildpostkarten.uni-osnabrueck.de/index.php>, [accessed 08 March 2017] (hereafter *HB*) or as a CD-ROM: *Der Erste Weltkrieg in deutschen Bildpostkarten*, Deutsches Historisches Museum (2002).
3 I would like to thank Dr May for his kind advice.
4 In 1907 there were at least 2,810 postcard companies in Germany; Christine Brocks, *Die bunte Welt des Krieges: Bildpostkarten aus dem Ersten Weltkrieg 1914–1918* (Essen, 2008), p. 45. At the same time in Britain there

existed at least 'many more' than 300 companies; John M. MacKenzie, *Propaganda and Empire: The Manipulation of British Public Opinion, 1880–1960* (Manchester, 1990), p. 22.

5 Ibid., p. 21.

6 Martin Willoughby, *Die Geschichte der Postkarte: Ein illustrierter Bericht von der Jahrhundertwende bis in die Gegenwart* (Erlangen, 1993), p. 10. Willoughby was an expert on postcards at the auction house Phillips in London.

7 Ibid., p. 13.

8 Christine Brocks, *Bildquellen der Neuzeit*, Historische Quellen Interpretieren (Paderborn, 2012), p. 68.

9 The 'Schutzverband für die Postkartenindustrie'.

10 Otto May, *Kaiser Wilhelm II. in der Postkarten-Karikatur: 'Herrliche Zeiten'?* Geschichte im Postkartenbild, (Hildesheim, 2013), 2, p. 132.

11 Anett Holzheid, *Das Medium Postkarte: Eine sprachwissenschaftliche und mediengeschichtliche Studie*, Philologische Studien und Quellen, vol. 231 (Berlin, 2011), p. 28.

12 Heidrun Alzheimer, 'Einführung', in *Glaubenssache Krieg: Religiöse Motive auf Bildpostkarten des Ersten Weltkrieges*, ed. Heidrun Alzheimer (Bad Windsheim, 2009), p. 15.

13 Stefanie Böß, '"Gott strafe England!" – zur Kriegspropaganda auf Bildpostkarten', in *Glaubenssache Krieg*, ed. Heidrun Alzheimer (Bad Windsheim, 2009), p. 223.

14 Ibid., p. 222.

15 Holy War: a war in the name of God – or even led by God himself.

16 Theresia Werner, '"Gott mit uns." Die Deutung des Ersten Weltkriegs im deutschen Katholizismus', in *Glaubenssache Krieg*, ed. Heidrun Alzheimer (Bad Windsheim, 2009), p. 72. See postcard from 1916, 'Mit Gott für Kaiser und Reich', *HB*, <www.bildpostkarten.uni-osnabrueck.de/displayimage. php?album=89&pos=139>, [accessed 18 November 2017].

17 Dominik Burkard, 'Mit dem Kaiser auf dem Weg durch die Zeit. Die Kirchen und ihr Selbstverständnis nach dem Kulturkampf im Kaiserreich', in *Glaubenssache Krieg*, ed. Heidrun Alzheimer (Bad Windsheim, 2009), p. 42.

18 Ibid., p. 50.

19 See postcard from 1915, 'Wir Deutsche fürchten Gott – Bismarck 1815–1915 – Sedan 2. Sept. 1870', *HB*, <www.bildpostkarten.uni-osnabrueck.de/display image.php?album=89&pos=61>, [accessed 21 December 2017].

20 Stefan Goebel, *The Great War and Medieval Memory: War, Remembrance and Medievalism in Britain and Germany, 1914–1940* (Cambridge, 2009), p. 289.

21 Burkard, 'Mit dem Kaiser', p. 51.

22 Werner, 'Gott mit uns', p. 74.

23 Pershing being the US general in Europe. See Jonathan Phillips, *Holy Warriors: A Modern History of the Crusades* (London, 2009), p. 328.

24 Reinhard Höhn, *Die Armee als Erziehungsschule der Nation* (Bad Harzburg, 1963), p. 189.

25 Ibid., p. 185.

26 Ibid., p. 230.

27 'Sedantag' was a memorial holiday in the German Empire celebrated to commemorate the victory in the 1870 Battle of Sedan. A few weeks after

the outbreak of the Franco-Prussian War, Napoleon III and his army were taken prisoner in the fortress of Sedan by Prussian troops.

28 Jochen Löher and Rüdiger Wolf, *'Furchtbar dräute der Erbfeind': Vaterländische Erziehung in den Schulen des Kaiserreichs* (Dortmund, 1996), p. 93. The Battle of Tannenberg was also linked prominently to the conflict in 1410 when the Polies and Lithuanians defeated the Teutonic Knights. See Goebel, *The Great War and Medieval Memory*, pp. 127–45.
29 Carl Erdmann, *Die Entstehung des Kreuzzugsgedankens* (Stuttgart, 1935), p. 141. In English, see Carl Erdmann, *The Origin of the Idea of Crusade*, trans. Marshall W. Baldwin and Walter Goffart (Guildford, 1977), p. 156.
30 Brocks, *Die bunte Welt*, p. 234.
31 Heidrun Alzheimer, 'Das Kreuz im Krieg', in *Glaubenssache Krieg,* ed. Heidrun Alzheimer (Bad Windsheim, 2009), p. 217.
32 Otto May, *Deutsch sein heißt treu sein: Ansichtskarten als Spiegel von Mentalität und Untertanenerziehung in der Wilhelminischen Ära (1888–1918),* Untersuchungen zu Kultur und Bildung, (Hildesheim, 1998), 1, pp. 393 and 395.
33 Ruth Diehl, Detlef Hoffmann, and Ingrid Tabrizian, eds., *Ein Krieg wird ausgestellt: Die Weltkriegssammlung des Historischen Museums (1914–1918),* Kleine Schriften des Historischen Museums, (Frankfurt, 1976), 8, p. 314, fig. 9/4.
34 Jonathan Riley-Smith, *Hospitallers: The History of the Order of St John* (London, 1999), pp. 127–28.
35 The tradition continues to the present; since 1999 Oskar Michael Hans Karl Prinz von Preußen has been the thirty-seventh Herrenmeister.
36 Process of Nazification by means of a system of totalitarian control and coordination over all aspects of society.
37 May, *Deutsch sein*, p. 395.
38 Ibid., pp. 446 and 451.
39 May, *Kaiser Wilhelm II*, p. 136.
40 Burkard, 'Mit dem Kaiser', p. 55.
41 See Jan Stefan Richter, *Die Orientreise Kaiser Wilhelms II. 1898: Eine Studie zur deutschen Außenpolitik an der Wende zum 20. Jahrhundert* (Hamburg, 1997).
42 May, *Kaiser Wilhelm II*, p. 132.
43 May, *Deutsch sein*, pp. 562–63.
44 May, *Kaiser Wilhelm II*, p. 40.
45 Ibid., p. 29.
46 May, *Deutsch sein*, pp. 562–63.
47 Specifically, of the Bailiwick of Brandenburg.
48 See Siberry, *New Crusaders*, fig. 8.
49 Ibid., pp. 67–68, and Christopher Tyerman, *The Debate on the Crusades* (Manchester, 2011), p. 140.
50 Walter Scott, *The Talisman* (London, 1825); in German, *Der Talisman* (Leipzig, 1826).
51 See Salvador Oberhaus, *'Zum wilden Aufstande entflammen': Die deutsche Propagandastrategie für den Orient im Ersten Weltkrieg am Beispiel Ägypten* (Saarbrücken, 2012).
52 For more postcards concerning the alliance between the Central Powers and the Ottoman Empire, see Otto May, *Weltkrieg in Postkarten, 1914–1918*, Geschichte im Postkartenbild, (Hildesheim, 2013), 4, pp. 152–54, figs. 367–74.

76   *Felix Hinz*

53 Friedrich Heer, *Kreuzzüge – gestern, heute, morgen?* (Luzern/Frankfurt, 1969), p. 183.
54 Alzheimer, 'Einführung', p. 20.
55 A postman estimated their percentage as 90%; Brocks, *Die bunte Welt*, p. 51.
56 Not so in Britain, where picture postcards played a major role in the Second World War and even later; MacKenzie, *Propaganda and Empire*, p. 23.
57 Willoughby, *Geschichte der Postkarte*, p. 120.

Bibliography

Primary

Ansichtskarten. Museum für Kommunikation, Berlin. http://sammlungen. museumsstiftung.de/ansichtskarten. [Accessed 8 March 2017].
Der Erste Weltkrieg in deutschen Bildpostkarten. Deutsches Historisches Museum. CD-ROM. 2002.
Historische Bildpostkarten. University of Osnabrück. www.bildpostkarten. uni-osnabrueck.de/index.php. [Accessed 8 March 2017].
Scott, Walter. *The Talisman.* London: Hurst, 1825. [German: *Der Talisman.* Leipzig: Herbig, 1826].

Secondary

Alzheimer, Heidrun. 'Das Kreuz im Krieg'. In *Glaubenssache Krieg: Religiöse Motive auf Bildpostkarten des Ersten Weltkrieges.* ed. Heidrun Alzheimer. Bad Windsheim: Verlag Fränkisches Freilandmuseum, 2009, pp. 214–20.
———. 'Einführung', In *Glaubenssache Krieg: Religiöse Motive auf Bildpostkarten des Ersten Weltkrieges.* ed. Heidrun Alzheimer. Bad Windsheim: Verlag Fränkisches Freilandmuseum, 2009, pp. 13–24.
Böß, Stefanie. "'Gott strafe England!" – zur Kriegspropaganda auf Bildpostkarten'. In *Glaubenssache Krieg: Religiöse Motive auf Bildpostkarten des Ersten Weltkrieges.* ed. Heidrun Alzheimer. Bad Windsheim: Verlag Fränkisches Freilandmuseum, 2009, pp. 221–28.
Brocks, Christine. *Die bunte Welt des Krieges: Bildpostkarten aus dem Ersten Weltkrieg 1914–1918.* Essen: Klartext Verlag, 2008.
———. *Bildquellen der Neuzeit.* Historische Quellen Interpretieren. Paderborn: Ferdinand Schöningh (utb), 2012.
Burkard, Dominik. 'Mit dem Kaiser auf dem Weg durch die Zeit. Die Kirchen und ihr Selbstverständnis nach dem Kulturkampf im Kaiserreich'. In *Glaubenssache Krieg: Religiöse Motive auf Bildpostkarten des Ersten Weltkrieges.* ed. Heidrun Alzheimer. Bad Windsheim: Verlag Fränkisches Freilandmuseum, 2009, pp. 41–60.
Constable, Giles. 'The Historiography of the Crusades'. In *The Crusades from the Perspective of Byzantium and the Muslim World.* eds. Angeliki E. Laiou

and Roy Parviz Mottahedeh. Washington, DC: Dumbarton Oaks Research Library and Collection, 2001.

Diehl, Ruth, Detlef Hoffmann, and Ingrid Tabrizian. eds. *Ein Krieg wird ausgestellt: Die Weltkriegssammlung des Historischen Museums (1914–1918).* Kleine Schriften des Historischen Museums. Vol. 8. Frankfurt: Historisches Museum, 1976.

Erdmann, Carl. *Die Entstehung des Kreuzzugsgedankens* (Forschungen zur Kirchen- und Geistesgeschichte, Bd. 6). Stuttgart: Kohlhammer, 1935. [English: Erdmann, Carl. *The Origin of the Idea of Crusade,* trans. Marshall W. Baldwin and Walter Goffart. Guildford: Princeton University Press, 1977].

Goebel, Stefan. *The Great War and Medieval Memory: War, Remembrance and Medievalism in Britain and Germany, 1914–1940.* Cambridge: CUP, 2009.

Heer, Friedrich. *Kreuzzüge – gestern, heute, morgen?* Luzern and Frankfurt: Bucher, 1969.

Höhn, Reinhard. *Die Armee als Erziehungsschule der Nation.* Bad Harzburg: Verlag für Wissenschaft, Wirtschaft und Technik, 1963.

Holzheid, Anett. *Das Medium Postkarte: Eine sprachwissenschaftliche und mediengeschichtliche Studie.* Philologische Studien und Quellen. Vol. 231. Berlin: Erich Schmidt Verlag, 2011.

Löher, Jochen, and Rüdiger Wolf. *'Furchtbar dräute der Erbfeind.': Vaterländische Erziehung in den Schulen des Kaiserreichs.* Dortmund: Westfälisches Schulmuseum, 1996.

MacKenzie, John M. *Propaganda and Empire: The Manipulation of British Public Opinion, 1880–1960.* Manchester: MUP, 1990.

May, Otto. *Deutsch sein heißt treu sein: Ansichtskarten als Spiegel von Mentalität und Untertanenerziehung in der Wilhelminischen Ära (1888–1918).* Untersuchungen zu Kultur und Bildung. Vol. 1. Hildesheim: Verlag Lax, 1998.

———. *Kaiser Wilhelm II. in der Postkarten-Karikatur: "Herrliche Zeiten"?* Geschichte im Postkartenbild. Vol. 2. Hildesheim: Verlag Franzbecker, 2013.

———. *Weltkrieg in Postkarten, 1914–1918.* Geschichte im Postkartenbild. Vol. 4. Hildesheim: Verlag Franzbecker, 2013.

Oberhaus, Salvador. *'Zum wilden Aufstande entflammen': Die deutsche Propagandastrategie für den Orient im Ersten Weltkrieg am Beispiel Ägypten.* Saarbrücken: AV Akademiker Verlag, 2012.

Phillips, Jonathan. *Holy Warriors: A Modern History of the Crusades.* London: Vintage, 2009.

Richter, Jan Stefan. *Die Orientreise Kaiser Wilhelms II. 1898: Eine Studie zur deutschen Außenpolitik an der Wende zum 20. Jahrhundert.* Hamburg: Verlag Dr Kovac, 1997.

Riley-Smith, Jonathan. *Hospitallers: The History of the Order of St John.* London: Hambledon Press, 1999.

Siberry, Elizabeth. *The New Crusaders: Images of the Crusades in the Nineteenth and Early Twentieth Centuries*. Aldershot: Ashgate 2000.

Tyerman, Christopher. *The Debate on the Crusades*. Manchester: MUP, 2011.

Werner, Theresia. "'Gott mit uns." Die Deutung des Ersten Weltkriegs im deutschen Katholizismus'. In *Glaubenssache Krieg: Religiöse Motive auf Bildpostkarten des Ersten Weltkrieges*. ed. Heidrun Alzheimer. Bad Windsheim: Verlag Fränkisches Freilandmuseum, 2009, pp. 68–91.

Willoughby, Martin. *Die Geschichte der Postkarte: Ein illustrierter Bericht von der Jahrhundertwende bis in die Gegenwart*. Erlangen: Karl Müller Verlag, 1993.

4 'Unity! Unity between all the inhabitants of our lands!'

The memory and legacy of the crusades and Saladin in the Near East, *c.*1880 to *c.*1925

Jonathan Phillips

Across the closing decades of the nineteenth century, and comfortably into the early twentieth, major changes in political and cultural life across the Near East offered the region's many interested parties tremendous scope to look back to, and to draw upon, their memories of the crusades. Contrary to earlier thinking it is clear that the Muslim Near East had not forgotten the conflicts of the medieval era and had indeed preserved an understanding of the crusading period down through the centuries.[1] It is also apparent that from the time of Napoleon's invasion of Egypt (1798) the weakening of the Ottoman Empire led European powers to exert a growing influence in the region. Events such as the French conquest of Algeria (1830) and from the 1840s the return of a significant Western presence in the holy city of Jerusalem (for the first time since 1244) being but two examples of this. Rising tensions between Christians and Muslims, such as the 1860 massacre in Damascus, were another part of the wider context. In such circumstances, the period under consideration here was a particularly fertile time for people in the Near East to see the history of the medieval crusades as a precedent for contemporary Western invasions. They also sought a role model in the form of Saladin, the man who recovered Jerusalem from the Franks in 1187, to emulate and to remind themselves that the crusaders had been defeated and expelled.

It is also relevant to note that some Westerners, including those taking part in military campaigns, living in the Levant or who were there as peaceful visitors to the area (especially the holy places of Palestine), chose to represent themselves as crusaders and regarded their own actions as being in the footsteps of crusading ancestors. In part this runs alongside, and is deeply intertwined with, a revival of interest in the medieval period and the crusades in Western Europe, both major subjects in their own right.[2] Such attitudes and actions acted only to reinforce and encourage the perceptions of people in the Near East. That said, in an era that saw such epoch-making events as the First World War, the Sykes-Picot agreement, the disintegration of the Ottoman Empire and the Balfour Declaration, it must be made clear that the memory of the crusades and the figure of the Sultan Saladin formed only a small – but, I would argue, potent – element in a very complex picture.

Responses to the intrusions of the Europeans saw ideological developments such as the emergence of Arab nationalism, Pan-Islamism and Pan-Ottomanism. Likewise, changes in cultural life – partially influenced, or driven, by Western models in theatre and fiction, for example – meant a growing use of the past, and sometimes the memory of the crusading past, to represent hopes and aspirations for the present and future. There was both an opportunity and a need to interpret and to understand what was happening, thus providing both a historical context and a possible way forwards. Jan Assmann writes that cultural memory is 'dependent on epoch and interests', and he continues: 'cultural memory relates its knowledge to an actual and contemporary situation [...] each contemporary context puts the objectivised meaning into its own perspective, giving it its own relevance.'[3] The past was ripe to be used, in this instance by an extraordinary array of players, not least because, as Paul Connerton notes, 'our images of the past commonly serve to legitimate the present social order', or, in this case, from an Arab and/or Muslim perspective, to contest or modify the existing social order.[4]

Nationalism encourages a narrative that creates a sense of shared origins, of the fêted deeds of noble predecessors and of the mutual experience of successes and failures. It forms a heritage to identify with and to construct an Arab national community, although this in itself was subject to nuance, regional variation and also the influence of religion. Arab nationalism often embraced indigenous Christian groups very warmly, but the basic environment in which it emerged was Islamic with the Prophet as a foundational, spiritual hero of the people.[5] Set against this framework, Saladin's reputation as a man of justice, mercy, religion and generosity provided a rich blend of exemplary behaviour for a huge range of politicians, writers and religious figures to extol and for the wider public to admire and to identify with as they looked to resist the new Western crusaders.

The British conquest of Egypt in 1882 was to some extent a manifestation of the continued decline of the Ottoman Empire. The events behind it were also a symptom of the rising tide of nationalist sentiment across the Near East as various peoples and lands sought to shake off outside control, be it from Ottoman Istanbul or, more particularly, Western powers. Such was the complex history of the region that this was not always a question of specific geographical regions looking to establish or re-establish themselves. Ethnic groups such as Arabs and Kurds aspired to assume their own authority as well. The rise of Zionism and the wish to restore a Jewish homeland was a further part of the equation.

In assessing how and where the memory of the crusades impacted upon the situation a wide range of source material is at hand. The emergence of numerous newspapers, evermore print publishing houses (a particular driver towards shared identities),[6] a blossoming of theatre and literature, the evolution of the Arabic language and a growth in education (meaning both formal schooling and academic endeavour) all made a powerful contribution to the de-localisation of society and the faster spread of ideas. Several of the key figures involved here were active across these media as we will see.

Fiction, newspapers and publishing

Arabic fiction writing is one genre that saw many changes, not least because in the past it had lacked a tradition of short stories and novels.[7] Given the Western presence in the region there was, especially towards the end of the nineteenth century, widespread translation of European fiction (initially from French, then English and Russian) with writers such as Dumas, Scott and Tolstoy enjoying considerable popularity. Walter Scott's *Talisman* was the highest profile crusading novel of the day, and it was readied for publication in the scientific and literary periodical *al-Muqtataf* as early as 1887. Such a format reflected the interest in the storyline with Saladin himself as a positive and prominent chivalric figure therein. The translator (and editor of the journal), the secular reformer Ya'qub Sarruf, changed the title to *Qalb al-Asad wa Salah al-Din* ('The Lion Heart and Saladin') and admitted to taking the liberty of 'omitting, adding and changing parts of this romance to suit his audience's taste.'[8] As we will see, Scott's *Talisman*-derived storyline proved highly pervasive and durable.

The medieval period was not simply presented in a fictional context. One of the earliest Lebanese newspapers was *Hadiqat al-akhbar*, or 'Garden of News,' which emerged in 1858. Very soon it featured a serialisation of the thirteenth-century author Abu Shama's work 'The Two Gardens,' a major account of the lives of Nur ad-Din and Saladin, the two leading protagonists in the struggle against the Frankish settlers in the Holy Land and the crusading invaders from the West. Manuscripts of the narrative had been copied many times down the centuries, but the decision to feature this text was likely made because it was of interest to the readership. The first printed version of Abu Shama's text was advertised in 1860, followed in 1871 by an Egyptian-printed version.[9] Texts by other medieval authors were still being copied in manuscript form during the eighteenth and nineteenth centuries, but this would change. Printed versions of several important medieval narratives appeared, and this facilitated the wider circulation of stories that concerned, amongst many other matters, Saladin and the crusaders: Ibn Khallikan's huge *Biographical Dictionary* from the later decades of the thirteenth century was printed in 1881; 'The Perfect Work of History' (*al-Kamil fil-Tarikh*) by the highly influential Mosuli writer, Ibn al-Athir, in 1885.[10]

The emergence of further newspapers in the late nineteenth century saw continued references to Saladin. In 1892 the enterprising Beirut-born Christian, Jurji Zaydan, started the monthly *al-Hilal* (which is still in existence today) with articles 'popularising Arab and Islamic heritage'. Such a remit meant the sultan quickly became the subject of an illustrated biographical piece in June 1894.[11] Zaydan was a dynamic figure with a prolific literary output, much of which concerned the study of history. Part of this interest came from his experience as a war correspondent. He was, in modern parlance, 'embedded' in the expedition sent to the Sudan to rescue General Gordon in 1884, and in the course of the mission his personal bravery saw him decorated by the British. Zaydan went to London in 1886 and spent time in the British Library researching Arabic history, and his Western-influenced critical reading of the sources marked a new departure in Arabic historiography.[12]

Zaydan wanted his works to be accessible and influential, and to show the achievements of the Arabs within Islamic history as well as learning from the past to improve the present.[13] His 1889 'History of Modern Egypt' (spanning the years 643–1879) was, however, keenly informed by his reading of the contemporary situation. The crusading era covered over sixty pages, and in essence he framed the narrative as a coalition of the people of Europe defeating and enslaving a divided Near East. He was scathing about the rivalries in 1160s Egypt that gave the Franks a chance to invade and he showed minimal approval for any alliances or co-operation between the Western Christians and the people of the Levant. Such a narrative inevitably required a degree of conflation and omission, notably in glossing over the awkward dealings between Saladin and Nur ad-Din that almost saw a civil war.[14] Instead, the two men appeared in a more positive relationship, principally to demonstrate the fear that the combined power of Syria and Egypt could generate amongst the Franks. The grandeur of Arab culture was also emphasised, best represented by its hero Saladin.[15]

Zaydan also authored a great many historical novels, a genre he firmly established within Arabic literature. He wished to popularise Islamic history through fiction to stimulate 'the desire of the public to read history and read it abundantly.'[16] Of his prolific output, two books are relevant here; the first being 'Saladin and the Tricks of the Assassins' (1913) which was also translated into Persian and Kurdish.[17] The second concerned Shajar al-Durr, the wife of al-Malik al-Salih who was the last senior male Ayyubid (Saladin's dynasty) to hold real power in Egypt, and her subsequent emergence as one of the few female rulers in medieval Islam. Her husband died in the course of the crusade of King Louis IX of France (the Seventh Crusade) with his captivity at Mansoura a high watermark of medieval Muslim victories over the crusaders.[18]

Theatre

Theatre became an especially powerful medium in the Near East towards the end of the nineteenth century. There was no tradition of drama in the Western sense of, as Badawi argues, 'the imitation on a stage by human actors or a story or situation through action and dialogue in verse or prose.' Nonetheless there flourished a huge, centuries-old seam of popular entertainments, partially influenced by shadow plays, often comedic or satirical in character and delivered in colloquial Arabic featuring verse and prose.[19]

French and Italian operatic and drama companies had performed in Cairo from the late 1820s, largely to Europeans or a Westernised local elite. By the 1870s, in the words of the founder of modern Egyptian drama Ya'qub Sannu', there was a wish amongst Arabs 'to promote civilisation, progress and the refinement of manners'. He established his own theatre troupe (which included women), and wrote a few of his own plays. Songs played a large part in these productions and some were in verse too, initially using classical Arabic. Western influences were also apparent through the works of Molière, or adaptations based on Verdi's opera *Aida*, Corneille's play *Horace*, Racine's *Andromaque* and various works of Shakespeare.[20] From around the 1880s, and always running the gauntlet of strict censorship from non-Arab authorities, political plays also began to appear on the stages of the Near East.[21]

Najib Haddad was responsible for a version of *Romeo and Juliet*, although it was heavily modified to give it local colour. In 1895, he staged a highly popular work, *Riwayat Salah al-Din al-Ayyubi*, a play much repeated in the years down to the First World War and beyond, as well as being printed in 1898. The influence of Scott's *Talisman* was manifest, although Haddad's verse and prose text steers strongly towards the sultan as the representative of, at the time, pan-Islamic, and later pan-Arabic, pride. Saladin is, unlike in the *Talisman*, the lead character, and through monologues and exchanges with his chief secretary 'Imad al-Din (who is not in Scott's book), can outline his own thoughts and then overcome the invaders. The book's celebrated scene – a disguised Saladin slips into the crusader camp to heal Richard – is safely preserved in order to show the cultural superiority of the Arabs and the sultan's personal kindness and wisdom. Aside from various performances in Egypt the play was toured in Algeria in 1913 and 1921, Tunisia in 1913 and Morocco in 1927, indicating its broad and enduring appeal across the Near East.[22] By 1932–33, a British academic surveying contemporary Egyptian theatre could describe this *Talisman*-influenced drama as 'a stock piece' still regularly wheeled out.[23]

One of Zaydan's rivals was Farah Antun, a Lebanese Christian who worked in Egypt from 1897. He set up his own bimonthly newspaper (*The Ottoman Community*) with a view to educating and reforming his readership. At first, he seemed to espouse the idea of a secularised Ottoman state, a popular choice for Syrian Christians, although one that set him against other nationalist groups such as Arabs and Turks. Conventionally enough, he saw the crusades as the origins of Western aggression against the Near East and wrote in such terms in 1900.[24] By 1909 he had veered towards Egyptian nationalism, believing that his former allegiance to a secularised Ottoman state was misplaced; criticism of the British became an overt element in his work. Finding lucrative employment in Egyptian theatre (some of his output is best described as 'light dramatic entertainment'), he was also responsible for a number of adaptations or translations from Western works, including those of Alexandre Dumas.[25] In 1914, however, Antun wrote a more serious piece, 'The Sultan Saladin and the Kingdom of Jerusalem', a work that engaged with contemporary issues, social and political, and reflected a growing sense of originality and nationalist activism in the theatrical community. He stressed the sultan's usual virtues of wisdom, loyalty and faith, but also his importance as a unifier and a liberator in the face of the deceit and greed of the invaders. The play begins with two acts in Cairo as Saladin decides to reject various Western ploys to draw him into political alliances. After hearing of Reynald of Châtillon's unilateral attack on the peaceful Muslim caravan he resolves to fight. Act three moves to a tent on the battlefield at Hattin where, almost inevitably, we have the execution of Reynald. In the final act (set in 1189/90) in front of the walls of the liberated city of Jerusalem, Saladin receives various envoys, including, in disguise, Maria, a sister of Reynald of Châtillon. This (mythical) figure makes a vain attempt to assassinate the sultan, and Saladin, displaying his customary mercy, duly releases her.

Antun gave the conflict a noticeable Islamic accent ('This victory comes from God, I am only his servant'), quite a change from the author's previously very secular stance; he also pushed a strong anti-imperialist line, calling for people to fight to the death rather than see any land occupied by a foreign power. Saladin's lines 'Jerusalem will remain ours forever, and our land will remain our land' reflect this, although there is also an echo here of the sultan's own writings (recorded by his secretary Beha al-Din ibn Shaddad) with his observation to Richard the Lionheart that the king may 'not imagine that we shall give it [Jerusalem] up [...] as for the land it is also ours originally.'[26] Antun's play ends with a cry: 'Unity! Unity between all the inhabitants of our lands!' A crowd floods onto the stage to acclaim this call, rallying around a theme that would become ever stronger down the decades. Maria, incidentally, gives a nod to understanding Saladin's high reputation in the West by saying that 'in the future, in times of peace as in times of war, he will have the same standing as Charlemagne, Caesar and Alexander carry for us.'

The play emerged (as we will see below) just after the Ottoman Empire had entered the First World War and Sultan Abdul Hamid II (ruled 1876–1909) called for a holy war against his enemies. The British in Egypt cut ties with Istanbul and established a protectorate under martial law. In such a context the authorities took a dim view of Antun's work and imposed strict censorship on the piece. It took a number of cuts to be allowed back on stage – the play was then performed in Egypt, Syria and Palestine.[27]

Saladin was not the only subject for plays that recalled the history of the crusades. Ibrahim Ramzi was another well-educated dramatist with experience of the Western theatre who translated a vast array of historical, scientific and dramatic (Ibsen, Sheridan, Shaw) works. He also wrote an important historical drama, 'The Heroes of Mansoura' in 1915, dealing with the defeat of the crusade of King Louis IX of France in 1250. This episode had been vividly recalled in the Near East at the time of Napoleon's invasion in 1798, and Ramzi deemed it an appropriate setting for his own piece.[28] This was an intensely nationalistic play, prompted directly by the British installation of Hussein Kamel as sultan of Egypt in December 1914 as part of their protectorate. Given its tone and these particular circumstances the work was suppressed until 1918. As well as successfully resisting the Western invaders the other main part of the storyline takes the fate of the last male of the Ayyubid line, Turanshah, and twists it firmly in the direction of contemporary concerns. In reality, soon after Turanshah succeeded his father as sultan, he managed to alienate most of his father's court and was murdered on the banks of the Nile. In Ramzi's play, he does indeed try to strike out on his own but is persuaded to see that the age of sole power is over and that he must consult his nobles; an appropriate message for the British to digest at the time.[29]

History books

Back in the heart of the Ottoman Empire, another driver of the image of the crusades, again with a measure of Western influence (albeit one soon turned towards particularly localised interpretations and contexts), was through the production of history books and textbooks for the burgeoning education system, itself underpinned in part by measures such as the Public Education Regulations of 1869.[30] As Gühe has written, 'textbooks represent a significant aspect of national mythology and thus also of national re-enactment via narration.' She continues, quoting Jeismann:

> The relevance of textbooks as historical sources is described in their description as "safes of national self-confirmation, self-justification and patterns of identification", which is why they can represent "an analysis of the consciousness of an epoch [...] as typical and representative sources".[31]

Given their potentially considerable distribution, the messages therein are worth taking note of.

In the final decades of the Ottoman Empire a number of books emerged that included coverage of medieval European history and the Crusades, in part utilising Muslim texts. An attitude perceived by Gürpinar as a blend of 'inherited Muslim prejudices towards Western Christianity and the nineteenth century positivist-enlightened Western (and predominantly French) historiography' meant medieval Europe was seen as both barbaric and corrupt. The crusades amplified these characteristics and participants were frequently described as bigoted, to the extent that this was their principal motivation to take the cross; such a view was in fact a mental disorder passed on to their children according to Sehbenderzade Ahmed Hilmi in 1908.[32] In contrast stood the tolerance of medieval Islam, and the fact that the Europeans learned much from the Muslims – a view that was, to a large extent, an importation from the Western Enlightenment. Thus, writers such as Ahmed Rasim (1908–10) outlined bigoted Christians observing a culture of tolerance in Islam, albeit in the context of aggressive wars of conquest.[33]

Namik Kemal was a prominent historian of the age, again someone who had spent time in France before he returned to Istanbul. He wrote the first modern biography of Saladin in the Near East in 1872, to some extent as a response to the Turkish translation of Frenchman Joseph François Michaud's imperialistic *Histoire des croisades* (1811–22). He wished to use Muslim sources to depict the sultan in his proper standing and placed the biography alongside those of Mehmet the Conqueror and Selim the Grim, two heroes of Ottoman history.[34] A few years earlier, in 1865, the first Arabic translation of a history of the crusades was published in Jerusalem and was in fact a French work by Maxime de Montrond, heavily based on the labours of Michaud and originally published in 1840. It was translated into Arabic by Maximos Mazloum III the Melkite patriarch of Jerusalem, Antioch and Aleppo, with suitable neutralisation of some phrases used by Montrond that would cause offense to the readership, such as 'barbaric', 'infidel' or 'false prophet'.[35] The first modern Muslim-authored crusading history ('Splendid Accounts in the Crusading Wars') by the Egyptian Sayyid 'Ali al-Harari (1899) is significant for taking on the subject as a distinctive topic in itself, rather than featuring as a part of wider narratives of Islamic history. He also makes considerable use of medieval Islamic sources, texts that as we have seen, were becoming much more accessible over recent decades. Taking a cue from the very top, the author quoted Sultan Abdul Hamid himself to make plain the parallels between the medieval period and his own times: 'Our most glorious sultan has rightly remarked that Europe is now carrying out a Crusade against us in the form of a political campaign.'[36] Pronouncements from the ruler of the Ottoman Empire himself, duly repeated in the newspapers of the day, must have had a considerable impact in driving home this point.

The Ottomans and Saladin

The Ottomans themselves had periodically engaged with the memory of Saladin down the centuries. For example, the important historian and official Mustafa Naima (1665–1716) drew a parallel between contemporary wars against the Russians and the Austrians and the earlier defeat of the crusaders.[37] His interest in Saladin was not just framed in terms of military history. Naima viewed Saladin as a magnificent exemplar for contemporary rulers: 'It is the truth that he served religion and the state in a way which has been granted to few other kings. Books of history are full to overflowing with honour and praise for that noble individual.'[38] Alongside these references to the medieval sultan's faith and justice, the multiple naval battles of the sixteenth and seventeenth centuries had a strong sense of a crusading enterprise and were certainly seen, by both sides, as being in a continuum with the earlier period.

In 1878, Sultan Abdul Hamid II commissioned a marble cenotaph to stand next to Saladin's thirteenth-century wooden tomb in his mausoleum in central Damascus. The Ottoman was clearly aware of the resonances borne by the medieval hero, and the inscription linked him to the Ayyubid ruler who defended his people and his faith against invaders. There was probably a need for Abdul Hamid to boost his image in Syria after defeat in the Russian-Turkish War of 1878 and to tie himself to this champion of the past. Equally, for him to judge this a worthwhile exercise he must have believed that Saladin had a sufficiently high profile in his own right to warrant making the connection. The cenotaph itself is of an Ottoman baroque style, a mark of modernity at the time, and it remains in situ today.[39]

From the early 1880s the sultan, who, it must be remembered, was also the Sunni caliph, embraced the idea of Pan-Islamism as he sought to draw his people together against the influences and the incursions of the West. A powerful voice in this call was Jamal al-Din 'al-Afghani' (d.1897). The roots of his 'interest in *jihad* and bitter opposition to the British' came from his time in India in the 1850s and 1880s, although this did not prevent him from later spending time in London, Paris and many other European capitals; he also travelled extensively in the Muslim world. Al-Afghani is described as a 'neo-traditionalist' who wanted national and then (especially) Islamic precedents for the reform and advancement of society, change sometimes prompted by Western influences.[40] A picture of the West as hostile and dismissive of the Muslims characterised his writing. Thus, a spirit that was seen as nationalistic and patriotic in Europe was, he argued, branded as fanaticism in the East; likewise, national pride in the West was seen as xenophobia in the Orient. He suggested that the Christian world, in spite of its divergence of races and nationalities, was united in a desire for the destruction of Muslim countries. He felt the crusades survived as if nothing had changed and argued that Muslim nations did not have the same rights as Christian ones in international law. Westerners claimed the alleged barbarity and backwardness of the Muslims as a justification for attacking and humiliating them when in fact they were smothering awakening and reform in the Muslim lands.[41]

In a letter of 1885 he sought to convince Abdul Hamid that he, al-Afghani, was the right man to rally the Muslims of the world to the sultan's leadership, calling for 'the banner of the unity of Islam' to draw people to religious war. As Keddie summarised, 'Afghani had come to think that the Islamic world could best be saved from the growing menace of European encroachments by an appeal from a charismatic leader, himself, to holy war.' It is somewhat incongruous that of the two exemplars he chose as inspiring religious figures to rally a people to war, one was the man regarded by some as the initiator of the First Crusade, Peter the Hermit. Al-Afghani wrote:

> and also at the time of the ranging of my thoughts in this field, the life of Peter the Hermit passed before my perception: The zeal of that indigent hermit and the resolution of that poor monk; how he took a cross on his back and traversed deserts and mountains and entered city after city of the Franks, and in every kingdom raised the cry: 'On to battle'; so that he became the cause of the Crusades and the kindler of those horrendous events. The flame of emulation was lit in my heart.[42]

Al-Afghani's messianic appeal did not receive the commission he hoped for, but a few years later he travelled to Istanbul where in 1892 the sultan made him the head of his Pan-Islamic bureau.

Of al-Afghani's associates, one of the most prominent was Muhammad 'Abduh (d.1905), with whom he edited the short-lived but influential Paris-based journal *al-'uwa al-wuthqa* ('the Indissoluble Bond') in 1884. Together they argued against the West trying to subdue Muslims by disseminating liberal ideas and they asked why their own co-religionists did not recognise the French as religious fanatics and the most zealous defenders of their faith. Furthermore, they also identified Prime Minister Gladstone as a fanatic whose spirit differed little from that of Peter 'the Monk', a figure who had evidently caught al-Afghani's imagination.[43] 'Abduh became the Grand Mufti of Egypt and head of the highly traditional al-Azhar University; his message was more peaceful than that of al-Afghani, aiming to work through educational and legal reforms. His 'Theology of Unity' referenced the crusades, albeit in terms of the medieval past and the West's perceived right 'to tyrannize over masses of men.' Through their time in the Near East, however, the crusaders acquired a much greater cultural knowledge which they then took back to Europe. In other words, it was the Orient that enabled the West to take a step forwards.[44]

Kaiser Wilhelm II

The place of Saladin as a hero of the Muslim world was to offer a bridge between the Ottomans and their European patron, Kaiser Wilhelm II. In 1898, as he sought to woo the Ottoman Empire, Wilhelm organised a major state visit to Istanbul and then on to Palestine and Syria. The centrepiece of his time in Jerusalem was the dedication of the new Protestant Church of the Redeemer, built on the site of the former headquarters of the Knights' Hospitaller. Wilhelm was closely involved with a revived Protestant Order of St John, and he wore the Order's insignia prominently on his chest;[45] indeed, he was often described as resembling, or portraying himself as, a crusader on his entry into Jerusalem.[46] A few days later, in Damascus, such attire was forgotten as he lavished praise on Saladin, the crusaders' great nemesis and the hero of the Islamic Near East.

During his time in Damascus Wilhelm and his advisors decided to see Saladin's tomb in the heart of the Old City. There, Auguste Viktoria, the *kaiserin*, laid a wreath (later appropriated by T.E. Lawrence of Arabia and now located in the Imperial War Museum, London) on the Ottoman tomb bearing a message in Arabic commemorating the arrival of one great leader in the presence of another. Wilhelm himself remained silent and spread his hands, a gesture interpreted by the local press as asking mercy for the dead. He then said that the sultan 'was the great sign of his time, because of his boldness, his justice and his noble nature.'[47]

Later that evening the imperial party attended a lavish dinner hosted by the local Ottoman governor. The British diplomat, William Shortland Richards, reported the Kaiser's words:

> I remember that I am now in a city in which once lived the greatest prince whose name is recorded in history, the valorious hero, who by his courage, his elevation and nobility of character and his devotion to his religion was an example in heroism even to his enemies. I refer to the great sultan Saladin of the dynasty of Ayyub when I think of this.[48]

There is little doubt that these episodes in Damascus, explicitly lauding Saladin's many virtues, helped to draw further attention to the sultan, and they were widely reported in the burgeoning Arab press in Syria, Lebanon and Egypt. Of itself this signifies that Saladin was a familiar figure to the readership. The newspapers did not need to introduce him or to explain who he was – his historical achievements were taken as known. A new Egyptian weekly, *al-Manar*, argued that Wilhelm praised Saladin because:

> William II is a warrior because he is the leader of the best army of the world. Salah al-Din was the best warrior of his time. It is typical of the man that somebody distinguished by something will pay respect to his equal, even if he is his enemy.

Al-Mu'ayyad suggested that Saladin's honourable characteristics attracted the emperor, notwithstanding the fact that the former was 'protecting and propagating Islam' and the latter was propagating Christianity.[49] In other words, Saladin's personality and deeds were seen and understood as a benchmark by contemporaries. The Kaiser – his performance in Jerusalem aside – was aligning himself with a familiar and attractive message.

Ahmad Shawqi, at the time described as a court poet for the Egyptian khedives and an Ottoman patriot (he was later an Arab Nationalist), wrote a piece in *al-Mu'ayyad* in which he said that after the first four rightly guided caliphs, no Muslims were more meritorious than Saladin and the Ottoman Sultan Mehmet (conqueror of Constantinople in 1453). He wondered how Muslim writers had been so tardy to awaken to their memory, although, given the context outlined above and his own visits to the West, perhaps this was a largely rhetorical question rather than a realistic assessment of the standing of these two heroes.[50] Shawqi was to write other poems that lauded Saladin as a heroic figure; notably in 1912 after the loss of three pioneering Ottoman airmen who were buried next to his mausoleum and in 1926 in a poem about the city of Damascus.[51]

The Kurds

The contemporary theme of national identity was taken up by another group, namely the Kurds. In the closing decades of the Ottoman Empire those pushing for reform focussed on Turkishness: Turkish history, literature and language. To some, this excluded the Kurds and their culture, and in response groups emerged who wished to emphasise their identity in the face of, as they saw it, a history of Ottoman domination. In 1898 exiles from the imperial regime in Cairo founded *Kurdistan*, the first Kurdish newspaper, subtitled 'A newspaper in the Kurdish language for the purpose of awakening the Kurds and for encouraging the study of the arts.' Education was seen as a vital tool for engaging with the modern world, and there was a desire to

Figure 4.1 Cover of issue 1 of *Rojë Kurd* newspaper, 1913.

delineate the Kurds as a separate group with a special past; in other words, a people with a long historical record, a powerful language (in need of revival at the time) and great leaders – most notably, of course, Saladin. Supporters of this concept set about establishing a Kurdish character from within, looking to develop and clarify their culture, history and language.[52] One group founded a newspaper, *Rojë Kurd*, to awaken these issues amongst their people (Figure 4.1).

The cover image of Issue 1 (1913) was an illustration of Saladin himself, actually using the portrait over his tomb in Damascus. The sultan was a great symbol of military strength, but a series of articles put him forward as a model character to inspire. Several years earlier a celebrated Kurdish poet, Sheikh Riza Talabani (d.1910), looked back to his childhood in a Kurdish principality ruled by the Baban dynasty, a situation that had ended with their overthrow by the Ottomans in 1847. He wrote of being free from the House of Osman and drew a link between the medieval hero and his own favoured family:

> Arabs! I do not deny your excellence; you are the most excellent, but Saladin who took the world was of Baban-Kurdish stock.[53]

The Treaty of Sevres in 1920 made provision for the creation of Kurdistan, a homeland for the Kurds, but within three years, when the Treaty of Lausanne set out the borders of modern Turkey, the idea had gone.

Zionism

Another powerful current in the Near East was Zionism, the movement to re-establish a Jewish homeland in Palestine. As this gathered momentum in the late nineteenth and early twentieth century (1897 saw the first Zionist Congress) there was growing concern across the Arab world. The rising number of settlements in Palestine engendered considerable opposition, and in one case a central theme in trying to resist one of these sites entailed invoking the achievements of Saladin. Shukri al-'Asali, the district commissioner of Nazareth, wrote widely in the Syrian and Istanbul newspapers under the pseudonym of 'Salah al-Din al-Ayyubi'.[54] In late 1910 he objected to the sale of an area of land to Zionists, and in his emotive opposition to the transaction and to the removal of the peasants who lived there he recalled that the area included the castle of al-Fula (La Fève to the Franks, about seven miles south of Nazareth), which Saladin had captured from the Franks back in 1187. In support of his case he even cited the thirteenth-century writer Ibn al-Athir, while a cartoon published in the Beirut weekly magazine (*al-Himara*, 'The She-Ass') shows Saladin threatening a caricatured Jew who pours gold into the hands of an Ottoman official while in the background stands the castle. Saladin is captioned as saying 'Keep away from this fortress you swindler, or else I shall set on you the armies of my descendants and you will not come near a fortress which I conquered with Muslim blood.' In response, the Jew states that money and bribery will prevail. Saladin's status as a hero for Muslims and Arabs means this was an early example of his symbolic use in the conflict between these groups and the Israelis.[55]

The end of the Ottoman Empire and events in Syria

By this time, events on a bigger stage were moving rapidly. In the summer of 1914 the Kaiser had suggested that the Muslim world should rise up against the 'hateful, mendacious and unprincipled nation of shopkeepers' and sought to foment holy war against the British in India and Egypt. On 2 November the Ottomans entered the war in alliance with Germany, and within a couple of weeks the Grand Mufti had declared a *jihad* against Russia, Britain and France. The faithful were promised 'felicity' if they survived and assured of a place in paradise if they fell as martyrs; an attack on the Suez Canal in January 1915 was the first (unsuccessful) manifestation of this alliance.[56]

The Allied campaign in the Near East and Allenby's entry into Jerusalem have been dealt with extensively elsewhere. Suffice to note that the general was very clear in his wish that the British government did not label his victory a 'crusade', not least because of the large numbers of Muslim troops in his army and, as we have seen, the fear of a Muslim response to the caliph's call to *jihad*. While the government initially went along with this by issuing a 'D' notice, banning such references, popular sentiment and the national press overwhelmed such a position and multiple outlets described the outcome in such terms.[57]

Notwithstanding Allenby's personal sensitivity, this overt symbolism obviously raised the profile and the perceived relevance of the crusades further. Events in Palestine, coupled with the Balfour Declaration (2 November 1917) and the disclosure of the Sykes-Picot document, which made provision for the Arab provinces of the Ottoman Empire to be divided into British and French areas of direct rule and spheres of influence, naturally brought the historical context to the fore.

This was especially the case in Syria. In late November 1917, Jamal Pasha, the military governor of Ottoman Syria wrote to Emir Faisal (son of Sharif Husayn of Mecca, leader of the Arab Revolt against the Ottomans in 1916) and to Ja'far al-Askari (the commander of Husayn's army) in an attempt to set up a separate Turko-Arabic peace deal. In quite pointed terms he expressed distress that the latter, having fought on behalf of the Turks early in the war, was now in revolt against the Ottomans and thereby aiding the British cause:

> I like to believe that you have chosen this course of action out of a pure desire to defend the rights of the nation to which you belong. But whatever may have been the customs and circumstances which have caused this evil to enter your heart, you should not forget that the British Army, commanded by General Allenby is today conquering Palestine which Salaheddin defended.[58]

Faisal strove to form an independent Syrian state, setting up an embryonic Sunni Arab government in Damascus.[59] A 'Council of Directors' was named to run internal administrative matters as the emir himself journeyed to France for the Paris Peace Talks from November 1918 to April 1919. In September, the British and French agreed that the former should evacuate its forces from the Syrian coast and Cilicia, leaving their holdings inland to the Arabs. The prospect of the British withdrawal (in effect moving along the Sykes-Picot agreement), provoked great unrest because it seemed to presage open conflict with the French. Hostility towards all Europeans was manifest on the streets of Damascus. A meeting of the Syrian National Congress in late October debated the situation with motions and speeches calling upon Syrians to conquer the western region of the country. Within days, a document based on this speech was distributed on the streets of the city and reproduced in newspapers across the Middle East. 'The First Call' attempted to rally the Arab people against the despotic colonising powers that sought to:

> Enslave the Arabs, to violate their women, to rob their money, to destroy their religion and to annihilate the Arab nation. See how the Jews who are enslaved and simple have risen now to demand Palestine, pretending it to be the land of their ancestors. Do you not wish to follow their example? Do you not want to safeguard the land of your forefathers who defended who defended her from the offence of the crusaders in the days of Salah ad-din? Why do you not stand in their faces now?[60]

It continued by citing contemporary examples of others standing up to colonial rule: Morocco, said to be defending her independence from the French; revolutions in Egypt and India; uprisings in Anatolia; ethnic resistance from Kurds, Tartars and Turks. The example of the

Italian popular leader D'Annunzio in seizing Fiume by way of trying to ensure that it came under Italian control was put forward as a model to emulate with regard to Western Syria; he was said to be opposing the decisions of the Paris Peace Conference. There was a powerful, even apocalyptic, tone in the document because the French and:

> every colonising power want[s] to sentence to death all the Eastern Nations whose population are Muslims. Every nation that does not defend her women will be done with. Every nation that does not defend her religion – the religion disappears [...] Down with the colonising powers! God is great, the country is in danger. Then it is your duty to obey the call. Revolution.

The potential threat posed by such an appeal was recognised in London as a copy of the document was sent from the Head of Intelligence directly to the Under-Secretary of State at the Foreign Office. It was pithily assessed as 'a most dangerous pamphlet [...] the writer is as able as he is dangerous.'[61]

The sentiments aroused by this situation were also apparent in an article published to commemorate the Prophet's birthday in a nationalist Damascene newspaper on 5 December 1919. It is striking to see the French so clearly identified as crusaders (something they had certainly done so themselves) and with all the negative connotations therein:

> Muslims do not regard the Prophet, much as they venerate him – as being more than a man and a prophet; and when they pray, they pray to God alone. The colonisers who have descended on Muslims, particularly the French, who boast of their descent from the crusaders, continue to suppose, as their fathers did, that the Muslims of Syria worship Mohamad and believe that their souls return to him after death. We have been told that when a certain young Muslim was saved from drowning, some Frenchmen who were on their way to occupy Syria, said: 'Why do you fear death, when if you died, your soul would go to Mohamed?' The youth smiled scornfully and explained the matter, after which he expressed his regret that the French, who claimed to have mastered every science, should continue to persist in such ignorance, and wondered how they could be so ambitious as to colonise a Muslim country and associate with Muslims, while they still have the same notion about them as their crusading ancestors in the Middle Ages.[62]

In the longer term, such calls proved ineffectual in spite of the proclamation of Faisal as king of the United Syrian Kingdom (Syria, Lebanon and Palestine) in March 1920. Within months the French under Gourad took control over Syria. The general himself had already described himself and the French as 'descendants of crusaders.'[63] Infamously, as he visited the Ayyubid sultan's tomb, he is said to have remarked: 'Saladin, we have returned.' Whether Gourad or one of his associates actually uttered the phrase is now quite seriously questioned, but true or not, by dint of repetition it was 'proven' and gained notoriety in the Arab world.[64] In 1958 and in 1960, for example, President Nasser of Egypt quoted it in speeches.[65] Faisal, meanwhile, after his expulsion from Damascus by Gourad, was being put forward to govern the British mandate in Iraq. T.E. Lawrence, who had played a major part in the Arab Revolt and been prominent at the Paris Peace Talks, encouraged his candidacy, not least by describing him as 'the greatest Arab leader since Saladin.'[66]

As the British implemented the mandate for Palestine set out at the 1920 San Remo conference, the subject of the crusades inevitably remained relevant. When Churchill in his capacity as minister for the Colonial Office visited in 1921, a memorandum presented to him made the point that the Palestinians had defeated the crusaders and forced them out of their lands.[67]

Turkey and Mustafa Kemal

The end of the war brought the defeat of the Ottoman Empire. We have seen that Saladin had been a figure invoked by the regime, and so it is interesting to observe him occasionally put forward in connection with the Turkish nationalist movement of Mustafa Kemal, the man who so ardently wished to remove the collapsing sultanate. At this stage a pan-Islamic solidarity was important, and in March 1921 a Kemalist newspaper prepared for the forthcoming Congress of Muslim Nations to be held in Ankara.[68] As a rallying call against Western crusader aggression – 'the invasion of the Cross and Capital' – it wrote that:

> The corporeal and spiritual European nations are apparently still not far from showing the extremely fanatical and implacable enmity towards Muslims as did the Crusaders of old [...] The call of the EZAN from the heights will be reduced to silence before the centuries old fanatical attack of the West and the crusaders' army [...] a labour which has lasted from the Middle Ages.[69]

To the Young Turks, Western Christian imperialism was not an ideology that could be reconciled with Turks and Muslims. Ahmed Riza, writing in 1922, regarded European imperialism as a 'modern crusade'; one with a prominent religious agenda.[70] The Turks were the people to fight off these invaders. Thus, in the contemporary context it was once more Christianity against Islam with, as the official history of the Turkish Independence War (1925) suggested, 'the Turkish nation as the first and last bastion against this occupationist drive.'[71] Kemal's successes in Anatolia brought him considerable praise elsewhere in the Near East, notably in Egypt, where the Islamic dimension to his struggle as a Muslim resisting Western domination played well in contrast to the supine Ottomans. In September 1922, rumours even circulated in Egypt that Kemal was going to start a *jihad* to liberate Egypt from the British.[72] Poets compared him to the Prophet's companion and great general Khalid ibn al-Walid and to Saladin.[73]

Conclusion

In conclusion, amidst a series of seismic political changes, the crusades stood as a powerful and accessible symbol of long-standing Western aggression against the people of the Near East. In the formal sense in which most present-day academics define the subject, the campaigns of the nineteenth and early twentieth centuries do not stand as crusades because they were not papally authorised expeditions in which participants received spiritual rewards. But, given the headline similarity of European invasions and conquests, coupled with some Westerners' prominent self-representation as crusaders, it was logical that this would be a potent memory to invoke and to weave around contemporary events. In the case of Saladin, the image of a great leader who drew people together under the banner of Islam and then defeated the invaders meant that the sultan was an ideal figure to emulate and to aspire to. The many attractive aspects of his character, as a man of faith, justice and mercy, all added to his allure. As an aside, the role of Saladin as a rallying point was particularly ironic given that, down the centuries, he was generally seen in a highly positive light in the West (and continued to be so).[74] In other words, this period marks a further phase in the continued traction of the memory of Saladin across a range of cultural, religious and institutional boundaries. Significant changes in theatre, literature, newspaper production, the writing of history books and education, set against the turbulent political context, created a platform upon which this historical continuum could be highlighted and perpetuated. The crusades and Saladin were flexible enough to be adopted by the emerging ideas of, for example, Arab Nationalism, Pan-Islamism and the Kemalist Turks. They could also continue to be used by the Ottomans, who, as noted, had periodically engaged with them in the past as well. This survey has attempted to indicate the attraction and the durability of both the crusades and of Saladin. In part, this also explains why such ideas continue to be a rich seam of material for those who seek support for an ever-greater variety of causes down to the present day.

Notes

1 Jonathan Phillips, 'The Memory of Saladin and the Crusades in the Near East from the Fifteenth to the late Nineteenth Centuries', in *The Diversity of Crusading*, eds. Kurt Villads Jensen and Torben K. Nielsen, 2 vols. (Odense, forthcoming 2019).

2 Mike Horswell, *The Rise and Fall of British Crusader Medievalism, c. 1825-1945* (Abingdon, 2018); Siberry, *New Crusaders*.

3 Jan Assmann, 'Collective Memory and Cultural Identity', *New German Critique* 65 (1995), p. 130.

4 Paul Connerton, *How Societies Remember* (Cambridge, 1989), p. 3.

5 Peter Wien, *Arab Nationalism: The Politics of History and Culture in the Modern Middle East* (Abingdon, 2017), pp. 1–3.

6 Benedict Anderson, *Imagined Communities: Reflections on the Origins and Spread of Nationalism* (1983), ch. 4.

7 With *The Arabian Knights* and the *maqama* genre as exceptions, albeit ones described as exerting 'a constraining rather than liberating influence.' Matti Moosa, *The Origins of Modern Arabic Fiction* (Washington, DC, 1983), p. 5.

8 Ibid., pp. 75 and 79.

9 Konrad Hirschler, *Medieval Arabic Historiography: Authors as Actors* (Abingdon, 2006), pp. 118–21; on the context of newspapers at this time, see: Ami Ayalon, *The Press in the Arab Middle East: A History* (Oxford, 1995), pp. 29–34.

10 Rashid Khalidi, *Palestinian Identity: The Construction of Modern National Consciousness* (New York, 2009), pp. 43–44; p. 223, n. 20.

11 Ayalon, *Press in the Arab Middle East*, pp. 53–54; Anne-Laure Dupont, 'Le grand homme, figure de la "Renaissance arabe"', in *Saints et héros du Moyen-Orient contemporain*, ed. Catherine Mayeur-Jaouen (Paris, 2002), pp. 62–63; 70–71.

12 Moosa, *Arabic Fiction*, p. 157.

13 Thomas D. Philipp, 'Approaches to History in the Work of Jurji Zaydan', *Asian and African Studies* 9 (1973), pp. 63–85.

14 Jonathan Phillips, *Saladin* (London, 2019).

15 Magda Nammour, 'La perception des croisades chez Jurjy Zaidan (1861–1914)', in *Chrétiens et Musulmans au temps des croisades: Entre*

100   *Jonathan Phillips*

l'affrontement et la rencontre, eds. Louis Pouzet and Louis Boisset (Beirut, 2007), pp. 141–61.

16 Quoted in Moosa, *Arabic Fiction*, p. 158.

17 Translated into English as: *Saladin and the Assassins*, trans. Paul Starkey (Bethesda, MA, 2011).

18 Translated into English as: *Tree of Pearls, Queen of Egypt*, trans. Samah Selim (Syracuse, NY, 2013).

19 Muhammad M. Badawi, *Early Arabic Drama* (Cambridge, 1988), pp. 1–30; Jacob Landau, *Studies in the Arab Theatre and Cinema* (Philadelphia, PA, 1958).

20 Badawi, *Early Arabic Drama*, pp. 31–67.

21 Landau, *Arab Theatre and Cinema*, pp. 120–24.

22 Wien, *Arab Nationalism*, pp. 41–42; Gilbert Meynier, *L'Algérie révélée: la guerre de 1914–1918 et le premier quart du XXe* (Geneva, 1981), p. 174; Badawi, *Modern Arabic Literature*, p. 402; Khalid Amine and Marvin Carlson, 'Islam and the Colonial Stage in North Africa', *Performance and Spirituality* 3 (2012), pp. 1–12.

23 Neil Barbour, 'The Arabic Theatre in Egypt', *Bulletin of the School of Oriental Studies* 8 (1935), p. 173.

24 Donald M. Reid, *The Odyssey of Farah Antun: A Syrian Christian's Quest for Secularism* (Minneapolis, MN, 1975), pp. 98–101; Badawi, *Modern Arabic Literature*, pp. 343–44.

25 Reid, *Farah Antun*, pp. 98–101; 126–29.

26 Behaal-DinibnShaddad, *The Rare and Excellent History of Saladin*, trans. Donald S. Richards, Crusade Texts in Translation 7 (Aldershot, 2001), p. 186.

27 Luc-Willy Deheuvels, 'Le Saladin de Farah Antun du mythe littérraire arabe au mythe politique', *La Revue des mondes musulmans et de la Méditerranée* 89–90 (2000), pp. 189–203; Wien comments that this possibly marked 'the introduction of these events [Hattin and the fall of Jerusalem] as a literary topoi in the Arab world,' *Arab Nationalism*, pp. 42–43.

28 Niqula le Turc, *Chronique d'Égypte 1798–1804*, ed. and trans. Gaston Wiet (Cairo, 1950), pp. 35–36, 44–45.

29 Badawi, *Modern Arabic Literature*, pp. 343–49.

30 Ekmeleddin Ihsanoglu, 'Ottoman Educational and Scholarly-Scientific Institutions', in *History of The Ottoman State and Society and Civilisation*, ed. Ekmeleddin Ihsanoglu (Istanbul, 2002), 2, pp. 361–512.

31 Ines A. Gühe, 'Crusade Narratives in French and German History Textbooks, 1871–1914', *European Review of History: Revue européenne d'histoire* 20 (2013), p. 368.

32 Dogan Gürpinar, *Ottoman/Turkish Visions of the Nation 1860–1950* (Basingstoke, 2013), pp. 81, 143.

33 Ibid., p. 144.

34 Ibid., pp. 80–81, 87; Carole Hillenbrand, *The Crusades: Islamic Perspectives* (Edinburgh, 1999), p. 593.

35 Iris Shagrir, and Nitzan Amitai-Preiss, 'Michaud, Montrond, Mazloum and the First History of the Crusades in Arabic', *al-Masaq* 24 (2012), pp. 309–12; Emmanuel Sivan, 'Modern Arab Historiography of the Crusades', *Asian and African Studies* 8 (1972), pp. 109–49.

36 Quoted in Hillenbrand, *Islamic Perspectives*, p. 592.

37 Bernard Lewis, *The Muslim Discovery of Europe* (London, 1982), pp. 165–66; L. Thomas, *A Study of Naima* (New York, 1972), pp. 78–83.
38 Ibid., p. 46.
39 Stefan Weber, *Damascus: Ottoman Modernity and Urban Transformation (1808–1918)*, 2 vols. (Aarhus, 2009), 2, pp. 241–42; Stefan Heidemann, 'Memory and Ideology: Images of Saladin in Syria and Iraq', in *Visual Culture in the Modern Middle East*, eds. Christiane Gruber and Sune Haugbolle (Bloomington, IN, 2013), pp. 60–63.
40 Nikki R. Keddie, 'The Pan-Islamic Appeal: Afghani and Abdülhamid II', *Middle Eastern Studies* 3 (1966), p. 61.
41 *Revue du monde musulman* 22 (March, 1913), pp. 183–85.
42 Keddie, 'Pan-Islamic Appeal', p. 55.
43 Josep P. Montada, 'Al-Afghânî, a Case of Religious Unbelief?' *Studia Islamica* 100/101 (2005), p. 215.
44 Muhammad 'Abduh, *The Theology of Unity*, trans. Ishaq Musa and Kenneth Cragg (New York, 1980).
45 Jürgen Krüger, 'William II's Perception of Sacrality', in *Baalbek: Image and Monument, 1898–1998*, eds. Hélène Sadler, Thomas Scheffler and Angelika Neuwirth (Beirut, 1998), pp. 89–95; Bernd Isphording, *Germans in Jerusalem, 1830–1914* (Jerusalem, 2009), pp. 25–47.
46 Edina Meyer-Maril, 'Der "freidliche Kreuzritter" Kaiser Wilhelm II. – Die Kreuzfah rerrezeption in der deutschen Kunst des 19. Jahrhunderts', *Tel Aviver Jahrbuch für deutsche Geschichte* 34 (2006), pp. 75–97 outlines the interest in the medieval period and the crusades in nineteenth-century German art.
47 Abdel-Raouf Sinno, 'The Emperor's Visit to the East as Reflected in Contemporary Arabic Journalism', in *Baalbek*, eds. Hélène Sader, Thomas Scheffler and Angelika Neuwirth (Stuttgart, 1998), p. 131. Wilhelm also paid for the chandelier that was eventually placed above these monuments in 1914; ibid., p. 133.
48 FO 195/2024, report of Consul William Shortland Richards, November 1898, TNA. The phrase cited by Ende, 'a knight without fear or blame, who often had to teach his adversaries the right way to practice the Art of knighthood [i.e. chivalry],' conveys the same message; Werner Ende, 'Wer ist ein Glaubensheld wer ist ein Ketzer? Konkurrierende Geschichtesbilder in der modernen Literatur islamischer Länd e', *Die Welt des Islams* 23/24 (1984), p. 83.
49 Sinno 'Emperor's Visit', pp. 132–33.
50 Ende, 'Wer ist ein Glaubensheld', p. 84; Wien, *Arab Nationalism*, pp. 38, 61. On Shawqi see also: Arthur J. Arberry, 'Hafiz Ibrahim and Shauqi', *Journal of the Royal Asiatic Society* 35 (1937), pp. 50–58.
51 Wien, *Arab Nationalism*, pp. 38–40.
52 Martin Strohmeier, *Crucial Images in the Presentation of a Kurdish National Identity: Heroes, Patriots, Traitors and Foes* (Leiden, 2003), pp. 18–26, 42–46.
53 Shayk Riza Talabani, 'The Baran Land' trans. in Cecil J. Edmonds, *Kurds, Turks and Arabs: Politics, Travel and Research in North-Eastern Iraq, 1919–1925* (London, 1957), pp. 56–57.
54 Rashid Khalidi, 'The Role of the Press in the Early Arab Reaction to Zionism', *Peuples Méditerranéens* 20 (1982), pp. 116–17.

55 Neville Mandel, *The Arabs and Zionism before World War I* (Berkeley, CA, 1978), pp. 88–92; Benjamin Z. Kedar and Denys Pringle, 'La Fève: A Crusader Castle in the Jezreel Valley', *Israel Exploration Journal* 35 (1985), pp. 164–79.

56 Neil Faulkner, *Lawrence of Arabia's War* (London, 2016), pp. 24–25.

57 See Eitan Bar-Yosef, *The Holy Land in English Culture, 1797–1917: Palestine and the Question of Orientalism* (Oxford, 2005).

58 FO 686/38, November 1917, TNA; Abdul Latif Tibawi, *Anglo-Arab Relations and the Question of Palestine, 1914–1921* (London, 1978), pp. 242–45; Eliezer Tauber, *Arab Movements in World War I* (London, 1993), pp. 152–55.

59 Daniel Pipes, *Greater Syria: The History of an Ambition* (Oxford, 1990), pp. 23–28.

60 'The First Call', FO 371/4185, 20 November 1919, TNA, pp. 139–42.

61 Ibid., p. 142.

62 FO 371/4185, WAAP 17, 19–23 December 1919, TNA.

63 FO 371/4186, December 1919, TNA; James Barr, *A Line in the Sand: The Anglo-French Struggle for the Middle East, 1914–1918* (New York, 2012), pp. 87–88; see more generally, Eliezer Tauber, *The Formation of Modern Syria and Iraq* (London, 1995).

64 James Barr, for 'Syria Comment', 27 May 2016, <www.joshualandis.com/blog/general-gouraud-saladin-back-really-say/>, [accessed 19 February 2018].

65 *President Gamal Abdel Nasser's Speeches and Press Interviews 1958* (Cairo, 1959) 20 March 1958, p. 129; also see *President Gamal Abdel Nasser's Speeches and Press Interviews, April-June 1960* (Cairo, 1960), 7 May 1960, p. 85; 8 May 1960, p. 104.

66 Barr, *Line in the Sand*, pp. 103–4.

67 Haim Gerber, *Remembering and Imagining Palestine: Identity and Nationalism from the Crusades to the Present* (Basingstoke, 2008), p. 180.

68 Umej Bhatia, *Forgetting Osama bin Munqidh, Remembering Osama bin Laden: The Crusades in Modern Muslim Memory* (Nanyang, 2008), p. 21.

69 Anita P. Burdett, *Islamic Movements in the Arab World, 1913–66* (Slough, 1998), 1, pp. 373–75.

70 Ahmed Riza, *La failite morale de la politique occidentale en orient* (Paris, 1922); Gürpinar, *Visions of the Nation*, p. 156.

71 Ibid.

72 FO 141/514/2, 1922, TNA.

73 Israel Gershoni and James P. Jankowski, *Egypt, Islam and the Arabs: The Search for Egyptian Nationhood, 1900–1930* (Oxford, 1986), pp. 46–47.

74 Margaret Jubb, *The Legend of Saladin in Western Literature and Historiography* (Lewiston, NY, 2000).

Bibliography

Archival materials

FO 195/2024, report of Consul William Shortland Richards, Damascus, November 1898, TNA.

FO 686/38, November 1917, TNA.

FO 371/4185, November 1919, TNA.
FO 371/4186, December 1919, TNA.
FO 141/514/2, 1922, TNA.

Primary

Abduh, Muhammad. *The Theology of Unity.* trans. Ishaq Musa and Kenneth Cragg. London: Allen and Unwin, 1960.
Beha al-Din ibn Shaddad. *The Rare and Excellent History of Saladin.* trans. Donald S. Richards. Crusade Texts in Translation 7. Aldershot: Ashgate, 2001.
Islamic Movements in the Arab World, 1913–66. ed. Anita L. Burdett. 4 Vols. Slough: Archive Editions, 1998.
Nasser, Gamal Abdel. *President Gamal Abdel Nasser's Speeches and Press Interviews 1958.* Cairo: Information Department, United Arab Republic, 1959.
———. *President Gamal Abdel Nasser's Speeches and Press Interviews, April–June 1960.* Cairo: Information Department, United Arab Republic, 1960.
Niqula le-Turc. *Chronique d'Égypte 1798–1804.* ed. and trans. Gaston Wiet. Cairo: Imprimerie de l'Institut français d'archéologie orientale, 1950.
Zaydan, Jurji. *Saladin and the Assassins.* trans. Paul Starkey. Bethesda, MA: Zaydan Foundation, 2011.
Zaydan, Jurji. *Tree of Pearls, Queen of Egypt.* trans. Samah Selim. Syracuse, NY: Syracuse University Press, 2013.

Secondary

Amine, Khalid, and Marvin Carlson. 'Islam and the Colonial Stage in North Africa'. *Performance and Spirituality* 3 (2012), pp. 1–12.
Anderson, Benedict. *Imagined Communities: Reflections on the Origins and Spread of Nationalism.* London: Verso Editions, 1983.
Arberry, Arthur J. 'Hafiz Ibrahim and Shauqi'. *Journal of the Royal Asiatic Society* 35 (1937), pp. 41–58.
Assmann, Jan. 'Collective Memory and Cultural Identity'. *New German Critique* 65 (1995), pp. 125–33.
Ayalon, Ami. *The Press in the Arab Middle East: A History.* Oxford: OUP, 1995.
Badawi, Muhammad M. *Early Arabic Drama.* Cambridge: CUP, 1988.
Barbour, Nevill. 'The Arabic Theatre in Egypt'. *Bulletin of the School of Oriental Studies* 8 (1935), pp. 173–87.
Barr, James. *A Line in the Sand: The Anglo-French Struggle for the Middle East, 1914–1918.* New York: W.W. Norton, 2012.
———. 'Syria Comment', 27 May 2016. www.joshualandis.com/blog/general-gouraud-saladin-back-really-say/. [Accessed 19 February 2018].
Bar-Yosef, Eitan. *The Holy Land in English Culture, 1797–1917: Palestine and the Question of Orientalism.* Oxford: OUP, 2005.

Bhatia, Umej. *Forgetting Osama bin Munqidh, Remembering Osama bin Laden: The Crusades in Modern Muslim Memory*. Nanyang: S. Rajaratnam School of International Studies, 2008.

Connerton, Paul. *How Societies Remember*. Cambridge: CUP, 1989.

Deheuvels, Luc-Willy. 'Le Saladin de Farah Antun du mythe littérraire arabe au mythe politique'. *La Revue des mondes musulmans et de la Méditerranée* 89–90 (2000), pp. 189–203.

Dupont, Annc-Laure. 'Le grand homme, figure de la "Renaissance arabe"'. In *Saints et héros du Moyen-Orient contemporain*. ed. Catherine Mayeur-Jaouen. Paris: Maisonneueve et Larose, 2002, pp. 47–73.

Edmonds, Cecil J. *Kurds, Turks and Arabs: Politics, Travel and Research in North-Eastern Iraq, 1919–1925*. London: OUP, 1957.

Ende, Werner. 'Wer ist ein Glaubensheld, wer ist ein Ketzer? Konkurrierende Geschichtesbilder in der modernen Literatur islamischer Lände'. *Die Welt des Islams* 23/24 (1984), pp. 70–94.

Faulkner, Neil. *Lawrence of Arabia's War*. London: Yale University Press, 2016.

Gershoni, Israel, and James P. Jankowski. *Egypt, Islam and the Arabs: The Search for Egyptian Nationhood, 1900–1930*. Oxford: OUP, 1986.

Gühe, Ines Anna. 'Crusade Narratives in French and German History Text-books, 1871–1914'. *European Review of History: Revue européenne d'histoire* 20 (2013), pp. 367–82.

Gürpinar, Dogan. *Ottoman/Turkish Visions of the Nation 1860–1950*. Basingstoke: Palgrave, 2013.

Heidemann, Stefan. 'Memory and Ideology: Images of Saladin in Syria and Iraq'. In *Visual Culture in the Modern Middle East*. ed. Christiane Gruber and Sune Haugbolle. Bloomington: Indiana University Press, 2013, pp. 57–81.

Hillenbrand, Carole. *The Crusades: Islamic Perspectives*. Edinburgh: Edinburgh University Press, 1999.

Hirschler, Konrad. *Medieval Arabic Historiography: Authors as Actors*. Abingdon: Routledge, 2006.

Horswell, Mike. *The Rise and Fall of British Crusader Medievalism, c.1825–1945*. Abingdon: Routledge, 2018.

Ihsanoglu, Ekmeleddin. 'Ottoman Educational and Scholarly-Scientific Institutions'. In *History of the Ottoman State and Society and Civilisation*. ed. Ekmeleddin Ihsanoglu. 2 Vols. Istanbul: Research Centre for Islamic History, Art and Culture, 2001–2.

Isphording, Bernd. *Germans in Jerusalem, 1830–1914*. Jerusalem: Palestinian Academic Society for the Study of International Affairs, 2009.

Jubb, Margaret. *The Legend of Saladin in Western Literature and Historiography*. Lewiston, NY: Edwin Mellon Press, 2000.

Kedar, Benjamin Z., and Denys Pringle. 'La Fève: A Crusader Castle in the Jezreel Valley'. *Israel Exploration Journal* 35 (1985), pp. 164–79.

Keddie, Nikki R. 'The Pan-Islamic Appeal: Afghani and Abdülhamid II'. *Middle Eastern Studies* 3 (1966), pp. 46–67.

Khalidi, Rashid. 'The Role of the Press in the Early Arab Reaction to Zionism'. *Peuples Méditerranéens* 20 (1982), pp. 105–24.

———. *Palestinian Identity: The Construction of Modern National Conscious-ness.* New York: Columbia University Press, 2009.

Krüger, Jürgen. 'William II's Perception of Sacrality'. In *Baalbek: Image and Monument, 1898–1998.* eds. Hélène Sadler, Thomas Scheffler and Angelika Neuwirth. Stuttgart: Steiner, 1998, pp. 89–95.

Landau, Jacob M. *Studies in the Arab Theatre and Cinema.* Philadelphia: University of Pennsylvania Press, 1958.

Lewis, Bernard. *The Muslim Discovery of Europe.* London: Weidenfeld and Nicholson, 1982.

Mandel, Neville. *The Arabs and Zionism before World War I.* Berkeley: University of California Press, 1978.

Meyer-Maril, Edina. 'Der "freidliche Kreuzritter" Kaiser Wilhelm II. – Die Kreuzfahrerrezeption in der deutschen Kunst des 19. Jahrhunderts'. *Tel Aviver Jahrbuch für deutsche Geschichte* 34 (2006), pp. 75–97.

Meynier, Gilbert. *L'Algérie révélée: la guerre de 1914–1918 et le premier quart du XXe.* Geneva: Librairie Droz, 1981.

Montada, Josep Puig. 'Al-Afghânî, a Case of Religious Unbelief?' *Studia Islamica* 100/101 (2005), pp. 201–20.

Moosa, Matti. *The Origins of Modern Arabic Fiction.* Washington, DC: Three Continents Press, 1983.

Nammour, Magda. 'La perception des croisades chez Jurjy Zaidan (1861–1914)'. In *Chrétiens et Musulmans au temps des croisades: Entre l'affrontement et la rencontre.* eds. Louis Pouzet and Louis Boisset. Beirut: Presses de l'Université Saint-Joseph Beyrouth, 2007, pp. 141–61.

Philipp, Thomas D. 'Approaches to History in the Work of Jurji Zaydan'. *Asian and African Studies* 9 (1973), pp. 63–85.

Phillips, Jonathan P. 'The Memory of Saladin and the Crusades in the Near East from the Fifteenth to the Late Nineteenth Centuries'. In *The Diversity of Crusading.* eds. Kurt Villads Jensen and Torben K. Nielsen. 2 Vols. Odense: University of Southern Denmark Press, forthcoming 2019.

———. *Saladin.* London: Bodley Head, 2019.

Pipes, Daniel. *Greater Syria: The History of an Ambition.* Oxford: OUP, 1990.

Reid, Donald M. *The Odyssey of Farah Antun: A Syrian Christian's Quest for Secularism.* Minneapolis, MN: Bibliotheca Islamica, 1975.

Riza, Ahmet. *La failite morale de la politique occidentale en orient.* Paris: Librairie Picard, 1922.

Siberry, Elizabeth. *The New Crusaders: Images of the Crusades in the Nineteenth and Early Twentieth Centuries.* Aldershot: Ashgate, 2000.

Sinno, Abdel-Raouf. 'The Emperor's Visit to the East as Reflected in Contemporary Arabic Journalism'. In *Baalbek: Image and Monument, 1898–1998.* eds. Hélène Sader, Thomas Scheffler and Angelika Neuwirth. Stuttgart: Steiner, 1998.

Shagrir, Iris, and Nitzan Amitai-Preiss. 'Michaud, Montrond, Mazloum and the First History of the Crusades in Arabic'. *al-Masaq* 24 (2012), pp. 309–12.

Sivan, Emanuel. 'Modern Arab Historiography of the Crusades'. *Asian and African Studies* 8 (1972), pp. 109–49.

Strohmeier, Martin. *Crucial Images in the Presentation of a Kurdish National Identity: Heroes, Patriots, Traitors and Foes.* Leiden: Brill, 2003.

Tauber, Eliezer. *Arab Movements in World War I.* London: Frank Cass, 1993.

———. *The Formation of Modern Syria and Iraq.* London: Frank Cass, 1995.

Thomas, Lewis, *A Study of Naima.* New York: New York University Press, 1972.

Tibawi, Abdul Latif. *Anglo-Arab Relations and the Question of Palestine, 1914–1921.* London: Luzac and Company, 1978.

Weber, Stefan. *Damascus: Ottoman Modernity and Urban Transformation (1808–1918).* 2 Vols. Aarhus: Aarhus University Press, 2009.

Wien, Peter. *Arab Nationalism: The Politics of History and Culture in the Modern Middle East.* Abingdon: Routledge, 2017.

5   The dead, the revived and the recreated pasts

'Structural amnesia' in representations of crusade history

Kristin Skottki

Many images and interpretations of the Middle Ages and of the crusades that were created in the eighteenth, nineteenth and twentieth centuries still haunt us today. As sedimented layers of interpretation they are hard to grasp due to the 'structural amnesia'[1] in historiographical praxis. The works they stem from are, as Benjamin Kedar put it, 'too recent to qualify as "sources" but too out-of-date to pass muster as "secondary literature".'[2] These academic images and interpretations derived their power, resilience and longevity from the claims of truthfulness, authenticity and objectivity their creators bestowed upon them. These medievalisms, I will argue, might – on a first glance – have left the consciousness of the academic community but are alive and kicking in the public sphere.

Reconstructing history

In my view, one of the most important insights from constructivist approaches to history is that history only exists if someone in the present tries to make sense of what happened in the past. History has no ontological status *per se*; it is a relational phenomenon based on the process of relating one thing with another; namely, the present with the past.[3] History is always an *attempt* to reconstruct the past as plausibly and truthfully as possible, but it is impossible to recreate the past in its entirety. It is therefore important to differentiate between *the past* and *history* – the first is what we are aiming to reconstruct, the second is what we are able to shape, to define and to 'make'. This understanding of history entails a number of hermeneutical challenges to the historicisation routine[4] and the representation of the past in general.

The understanding of history as a relational phenomenon calls our attention to the substantial connection between the historian and the historical record enabling the (re)creation of history, or the production of historiography. It is, after all, the evidence that bridges the gap between past and present – the sources in their materiality and mediality are witnesses of the past, but they are present; they are part of the 'then' and the 'now' at the very same time. This argument actually has two sides: on the one hand, the limits of an appropriate historical reconstruction are first and foremost set by the available source material, and how we choose to engage with it. Even the simplest and most 'innocent' research question already co-determines which source material is read in which ways and therefore channels the way history is presented in a given historical reconstruction. This point cannot be overstressed: the historical artefacts and evidence (which we are used to calling 'sources') are our only access and medium to make qualified statements about the past. But the source material does not speak by itself; it demands to be interpreted, translated and contextualised – it is the historian's task to turn different sorts of evidence into sources of historical knowledge and understanding.

On the other hand (and as a consequence of the abovesaid), representations of the past are inevitably governed by the interests, agendas and perspectives of the scholars who try to reconstruct a given historical phenomenon. This is not to say that every historian is automatically under suspicion of letting an ideological bias govern his or her work. For the sake of my argument it is important to differentiate between *perspective, (research) interests* and *agenda* on the one side as epistemological prerequisites for any kind of intellectual labour and *ideology* on the other side as a set of value judgements and opinions which are presented as self-evident and 'objective' but which all too often stem from a lack of hermeneutical self-reflexivity. From a constructivist point of view, plausibility and appropriateness of a historical representation may indeed only be achieved by disclosing the 'situatedness' (*Standortgebundenheit*) of one's own hermeneutical presuppositions and the composition of one's toolbox for historical reconstruction.

Unfortunately, one important feature of the self-legitimization of history as an academic field (or even science) in the age of historicism was to disguise this situatedness of historical reconstructions by formulating definitive claims of truth and denying the role of the research subject in creating the research object. The historicist ideals of objectivity[5] and detachment obscured at least three fundamental connections:

1   the connection between the historical artefacts and evidence (the 'sources') and those who use them to reconstruct history;
2   the connection between the academic historian and the surrounding world – be it the academic community, the nation or society in general; and

3   the connection between the layers of interpretation – synchronic and diachronic.

With regards to the third point, one may recall the still common historiographical practice to securely store older and concomitant differing interpretations into a chapter called 'state of research'. This conveys the impression as if every historian reconstructs his research object from scratch and writes the 'new', 'better', or 'real' history, solely committed to the presumably pristine original sources. But as this chapter will show, 'reconfigured' and residual older interpretations (diachronic layers), other disciplinary perspectives as well as explanatory models derived from other fields (synchronic layers) can be identified as the major challenges and provocations which crusade historiography has to deal with today. The 'structural amnesia' inherent to historicism, obliterating the connections and continuities on the three above-named levels, may be identified as one of the major causes for the fierce struggle over the meaning and nature of the crusades today.

Challenging the temporal gap

If one takes the strong connection between history and present seriously, it is no wonder that assertions and judgements about the past are always (but often only implicitly) formulated as comparisons – between now and then, 'us' and 'them'. This means that representations of the past (i.e. history) are by nature also statements about the present. Richard Utz called our attention to the very meaning of the word representation: it is re-*present*-ation (*Ver-gegen-wärtigung*; 'making present again').[6] History, if understood as a form of representation, *per se* challenges the gap between past and present as in the 'historical consciousness' (*Geschichtsbewusstsein*) of a society, community or even an individual a variety of spatialities and temporalities – that is timescapes – are present, or rather made present again.[7]

This understanding of history questions some of the fundamental premises of historicism. As Glenn W. Most has shown, one of the basic practices of Historical Studies is to highlight discontinuities and to construct otherness/alterity as a necessary step to establish a temporal gap between the present and the past:

[W]hat is specific to the act of historicization is that it resituates the defamiliarized element within the context of its origin and asserts that its essence is determined by where it came from historically, its moment of origin. This removal of an element from the present and its recontextualization within the situation of its origin creates a temporal gap between two moments, the present in which one finds oneself and the past which one has reconstituted as an origin. Such a gap inevitably creates a pressure to develop narratives which could bridge the distance between that past and this present, both small narratives about the particular situation of the origin in which the questionable element came about and larger narratives linking that origin to the present.[8]

In common historiographical practice, a point of origin for a given historical phenomenon is identified (or rather, created), which is then fetishized[9] not only as a beginning but even as the essence of the thing.[10] This fetishized origin (or the 'Idol of Origins', as Marc Bloch called it)[11] is then used to judge the status as 'real', 'invented', 'pseudo-'or 'para-' (etc.) of later phenomena and developments. But it is also used to judge the appropriateness and plausibility of academic and popular representations of the past. This rupture, then, paradoxically creates three different pasts that I would like to label in the following way: the *dead past* encapsulated in the historical source material; the *revived pasts* of memories, imaginations and re-enactments of historical events that still (or again) surround us today; and the *recreated pasts* of historical reconstructions.

The expression *revived pasts* highlights the performative and constructed character of 'historical culture' (*Geschichtskultur*) deliberately to challenge the common belief that 'memories' of historical events are something naturally inherited and passed on from generation to generation in some biological or even genetic way. 'Historical culture' refers to every kind of engagement with and representation of the past in the public and private sphere, but generally outside of academia. The expression *revived pasts* is a deliberate plural because, as already mentioned above, the historical consciousness of a given society relates to a multitude of different timescapes and layers of history, and the composition of these historical imaginations can change dramatically over the course of time. Similarly, the expression *recreated pasts* is also plural as the sciences and humanities in general, and historiography in particular, are based on the principles of continuous revisionism.[12] The constant process of disproving some and verifying other historiographical representations and interpretations naturally produces a variety of academic recreations of the dead past.

The main obstacle for understanding the consequences of this interrelatedness of the different pasts seems to stem from the reluctance of academic historians to acknowledge their part in producing recreated pasts and facilitating (at least some parts of) the revived pasts.

Fortunately, the field of medievalism studies tries to close this gap. Utz recently defined medievalism in this way:

> Medievalism is the ongoing and broad cultural phenomenon of reinventing, remembering, recreating, and reenacting the Middle Ages. Medieval Studies, the academic study of medieval culture focused on establishing the 'real' Middle Ages, is one essential contributor to the cultural phenomenon of Medievalism.[13]

This is indeed a provocative statement as it links two fields which were deliberately separated in the nineteenth century.[14] But Utz is right – there is no clear-cut, consistent difference between academic historical studies or, in this case, Medieval Studies (*Mediävistik*) and historical culture or, in this case, medievalism (*Mediävalismus*). It is indeed one of the most urgent claims of Utz's 'Manifesto for Medievalism' that professional historians should not only engage with historical source material – the *dead past* – but also with the *revived pasts*; and acknowledge how both influence the way in which they engender the *recreated pasts*.[15]

Recently, a number of scholars are engaged in studying what Mike Horswell has named 'crusader medievalism'.[16] For decades, Jonathan Riley-Smith, his pupil Elizabeth Siberry and Adam Knobler were almost the only scholars studying the afterlife, memory and attempts of revitalising the crusades in post-medieval times.[17] The publication of this series, as well as blogs, workshops, conferences and conference sessions being organised last year and this year (2018), show that an increasing number of scholars, not only crusade historians, identify the appropriation of crusade images and rhetoric in post-medieval times, and especially in the present, as worthy objects of historical study. Finally, students of medieval history and medievalism are coming together.

But again, the acknowledgment of the intermingling of these three different pasts entails a number of hermeneutical challenges. The first challenge lies in the observation that different forms of representations of and engagements with the past in 'historical culture' have often been labelled as 'memories', leading to many epistemological and methodological confusions and inaccuracies. Kerwin Klein called our attention to the fact that:

> for years, specialists have dealt with such well-known phenomena as oral history, autobiography, and commemorative rituals without ever pasting them together into something called memory. Where we once spoke of folk history or popular history or oral

history or public history or even myth we now employ memory as a metahistorical category that subsumes all these various terms.[18]

Wulf Kansteiner has also demanded a reflective handling of concepts like 'collective memory', 'trauma' etc. and sought to:

> conceptualize collective memory as the result of the interaction among three types of historical factors: the intellectual and cultural traditions that frame all our representations of the past, the memory makers who selectively adopt and manipulate these traditions, and the memory consumers who use, ignore, or transform such artifacts according to their own interests.[19]

It is also worth noting that Kansteiner too observes a blurring of the line between academic historiography (*recreated pasts*) and collective memories (or *revived pasts*), if history is understood as a mediated phenomenon. One may conclude that scrutinising representations of the past in academic historiography needs to take into account the three above-named historical factors, albeit in a modified manner: the common and accepted modes of narrating and representing the dead past in historiographical accounts; the historians, who claim to represent the dead past as accurately as possible; and the academic and non-academic readership, who might either trust in the expertise of the academic historian and his recreation of the past – or not.

The second challenge lies in the traditional understanding of the function of the historicisation routine. It may also – but not exclusively – be understood as a way to cope with the revived pasts; many historians who engage with popular images of history, of the Middle Ages and especially of the crusades, understand themselves as 'mythbusters'.[20] Metaphorically speaking, historians may also be understood as gravediggers of revived pasts which they try to render harmless by turning them into history (the dead past) – something that might be a worthy object of knowledge but which has no reality or ontic status in the present.[21] A phenomenon like the crusades, in this traditional sense, needs to be a dead thing before it can be turned into a worthy object for historical research. Some point in the past needs to be identified where it changed status from being a live/vivid social reality to being a memory – when it changed status from being medieval to being 'a medievalism'. Therefore, it is no wonder how sensitive historians often are when they are confronted with revived pasts outside of academia, as these 'lively' pasts seem to question and challenge the historians' interpretational sovereignty over the dead past.[22]

This observation is closely tied to the third challenge: the role of the public intellectual. While in theory it may sound plausible to differentiate between revived pasts in historical culture and recreated pasts in academic historiography, this division is, in reality, a fallacy. It is part of the job description of most current professorships to engage with the so-called 'third mission'; that is, to transmit and translate academic findings to society in general and to actively seek exchange with non-academic partners.

The real challenge for historians (and academics in general) lies exactly in the proximity and entanglement of academic historical research on the one side and different forms of collective and individual engagement with the revived pasts on the other. The academic field of Medievalism Studies is itself a flagship for the strong connection between Medieval Studies (here as Crusade Studies) and medievalisms (as crusader medievalism).[23] The self-image (and illusion) of nineteenth-century historicism as being completely detached from the contemporary world, as well as the fears of loss of relevance for public discourse which seem to have haunted Medieval Studies at least since the beginning of the twentieth century, form the basis for underestimating how much academic interpretations and scholarly expertise actually matter in the public sphere.

At least with a topic like the crusades, that has gained so much interest and relevance in the public sphere within roughly the last twenty years (see below), medievalists have finally received the attention they desired. The different ways in which non-academic audiences sometimes adopt and process the scholarly output may not always be what academics had hoped for, but it would be a dangerous fallacy to believe the recreated pasts would have no influence on the revived pasts.

The resurgence of the crusades

As stated above, the status, relevance and visibility of certain historical events and developments in the historical consciousness of a given society might change dramatically over the course time. Something that has changed profoundly within roughly the last twenty years is the representation of crusade history. At least three major developments that have shaped this change can be identified.

The first is an academic one though, of course, not free of external influences. With the advancement of the neo-religious explanation of the crusades since the late 1970s, which to large parts can be credited to Jonathan Riley-Smith and his school,[24] many general assumptions about and older interpretations of crusade history could be disproven and were abandoned inside Crusade Studies. Although the Riley-Smith school dominates the field, there nevertheless exist at least four rough groups who do not agree over such basic characteristics of the crusades as their temporal and spatial limits or their scope, in regard to who and what is identified as their target.[25] This major wave of revisionism has, since the 1970s, not only given room to a variety of explanations and interpretations in Crusade Studies but also to a culture of lively debates over the appropriate understanding of almost every single aspect of crusade history; not least because crusade scholars scrutinise this history from a variety of disciplinary perspectives, for example religious history, archaeology, art history, social history, literary studies etc.

The second major source of influence for the change in representations of crusade history may be found in the political, social and cultural reality since at least the 1990s, beginning with the end of the Cold War and the return of religiosity and religiously legitimised actions in the public sphere. But most importantly are the violent actions, wars and terrorist attacks since 2001 which are framed by public references to the crusades. On the one side we find, for example, the members of al-Qaeda, or since 2014 members of so-called IS (ISIL/ISIS), legitimising their terrorist attacks and military expansions as righteous *jihads* against their enemies, whom they call 'Crusaders', 'Crusader-Colonialists' or 'Crusader-Zionists'; as do the propagators of 'Virtual Jihadism'.[26] On the other, we find examples ranging from former US President George W. Bush calling the 'War on Terror' in 2001 a crusade; to Islamophobic 'Online Crusaders' in the West demanding a new crusade ('counter*jihad*') against Islam; and, finally, examples of White Supremacists such as Norwegian Anders Behring Breivik, who in 2011 legitimised his terrorist attacks with a number of references to the crusades as necessary wars against Islam and multiculturalism.[27] In all of these examples the crusades are called upon as revived pasts – or in the view of those who use these references, even as continuing pasts.

The third development might be seen in the (again) growing number of media representations of the crusades. Highly popular cultural appropriations of crusade history could be found in film (notably Ridley Scott's *Kingdom of Heaven* from 2005), in novels (especially Dan Brown's *The Da Vinci Code* from 2003, with Ron Howard's film version from 2006)[28] and in computer games (particularly *Assassin's Creed* since 2007).

But even with these examples cracks form in the carefully erected wall between revived pasts and academically recreated pasts. Crusade historians and historians of Christian-Muslim relations were in great demand to explain to a general audience the apparent connection between the medieval crusading past and present atrocities committed in the name of Allah after 9/11.[29] A number of well-known crusade scholars also reviewed and commented on those popular films and books in newspapers and magazines.[30] But the development also worked in reverse – almost every introduction or textbook on the crusades that appeared after 9/11 contained at least a short comment on the recent situation, while the above-named films and novels turned into worthy subjects of historical scrutiny in Medievalism Studies.[31] Most importantly, the general accessibility of social networking sites, social media sites, blogs and video sharing sites has made academic knowledge as well as popular representations of crusade history accessible to anyone who may be interested in this, but also enabled non-experts to voice and share their opinions with these different forms of representations.

The point here is that crusading images and rhetoric in historical culture, like in computer games, Hollywood movies, politicians' statements, internet blogs and chats, generated by more or less well-informed contemporaries, do not come out of the blue. While some of the producers and consumers of these images and rhetoric may indeed only be interested in utilising 'metaphorical memories'[32] of the crusades for their own purposes with no deeper interest in history, it is likely that a large proportion of these people endeavour to verify and authenticate information by searching for reliable sources. Those sources now can differ dramatically according to what the person believes to be reliable – is it the academic expert, who is also able to reach a larger audience through bestseller books, newspaper articles, a personal blog or his Facebook and twitter accounts? Or is it the internet platforms, where a peer group gathers to mutually confirm already existing opinions and world views, mostly conspiracy theories? Again, a clear-cut division of these two spheres does not exist. For example, in October 2017, George Washington University hosted a one-day symposium on 'The Middle Ages, the Crusades & the Alt Right.' The organisers of the workshop (Matthew Gabriele, Bruce Holsinger and Amanda Steinberg) created a Twitter hashtag (#AltCrusade17) for sharing live updates from the conference room, but this hashtag was hijacked by self-proclaimed 'Online Crusaders' (or however we want to call them), deluging the conference Twitter feed with memes, images and snappy patter celebrating their vision of the crusades as a just and holy war against Islam.[33] This might be a disturbing but all the more telling example of how easily and quickly academic discussions may nowadays reach a wider public, albeit in unpleasant ways.

The concurrence of these three developments – crusader rhetoric as a frame for terrorist attacks and hate speech, the growing interest in crusade history inside and outside academia and the interactivity of sharing and creating representations of the crusades via the World Wide Web in the first decade of the twenty-first century – accelerated the process of turning crusade history into a revived and vibrant past within the historical consciousness of Western and Islamicate societies again. But tracing the roots of this historical conjunction may also help to understand that this is not the product of a centuries-old continuity; rather, it is the product of the mutual processes of reviving and recreating the crusading past. Therefore, it is no wonder that crusader medievalism is now identified by many as a worthy object of historical scrutiny. Nevertheless, we should keep in mind the quoted caution by Kansteiner that a careful analysis of collective memories – or in this case, crusader medievalisms – in the present needs to differentiate between very different sorts of engagements with and representations of crusade history, as well as between very different groups of producers and consumers within the field of memory production and academic knowledge production alike.

Haunting the blind spots of contemporary historiography

These epistemological and methodological challenges will now be illustrated with a few examples. This is not an attempt to denounce the work of colleagues but may encourage a scholarly debate about how to engage with recent phenomena of crusader medievalism and crusade history alike.

Very recently, Andrew B.R. Elliott published the most comprehensive and pertinent study about images of the Middle Ages (i.e. medievalism) in today's politics and mass media; five of his eight essays explicitly dealt with the appropriation of the crusades.[34] His subject was in most cases the legitimisation of acts of violence with references to the crusades (or medieval history in general):

> [M]y suggestion is that even the most unpleasant or extremist ideology can be rendered banal by being shrouded within medievalism, used in an unthinking capacity without direct reference to the Middle Ages. [...] In all cases, as I will show, even when the so-called Islamic State consciously tries to recall a medieval Caliphate, these medievalisms are nevertheless banal in the sense that they mask a poisonous distortion of history for presentist concerns. Their concerns, like al Qaeda before them, are not historical, but ideological: they engage, therefore, not with history but use the past as a kind of buffet from which they can select the most palatable morsels.[35]

That said, it seems odd to expect terrorist organisations such as al-Qaeda or IS/ISIS to engage with history like a research centre. *Of course* they are using history only to serve their presentist concerns and goals; *of course* they cut out bits and pieces of history that seem helpful in justifying their self-fashioning as the righteous avengers of the orthodox Muslim *umma*.

It is, therefore, crucial to establish first a methodological toolbox for studying such examples of crusader medievalism, as by applying a number of insights from the field of memory studies or constructivist history, Elliott might not have projected such high expectations of historical accuracy onto terrorists. The categorisation of these crusading images and rhetoric as 'banal medievalism' or even 'empty signifiers' seems to belittle crusader medievalism in political and violent contexts, but also sets up an unnecessary idealisation of Medieval or Crusade Studies as the stronghold of the authentic and 'real' Middle Ages and crusades.[36] This is more surprising as Elliott repeatedly cites Bruce Holsinger's essay 'Neomedievalism, Neoconservatism, and the War on Terror', which warned academic Medieval Studies how images the scientific community creates of the Middle Ages can be – and already are – instrumentalised by politicians, policy advisers and, not to forget, perpetrators of violence.[37]

It may seem appropriate for historians to distance themselves from such revived pasts in political and violent contexts because these visions of history are used to harm people in the present. But the methodological approach to judge these sorts of crusader medievalisms by the standards of historical accuracy alone seems not at all helpful to me. This criticism pertains to all those historians who comment on non-academic forms of crusader medievalism as Elliott has, even on medievalisms which do not even *claim* to be historically appropriate (like any kind of fictional representation). Instead of just stating that al-Qaeda's or IS/ISIS's visions of the crusading past are ideologically motivated distortions (which they undoubtedly are), it might be more profitable to ask *why* and *how* they appropriate certain images (and others not) to serve *which purposes* in the given historical context of the early twenty-first century. Another important aspect would be to ask why they are able to convince certain people and groups of the truthfulness of their evidently ideological distortions of the past.

At the same time, we should be careful in judging something as ahistorical and non-referential just because *we* might not be aware of the underlying connection. Just as an example, one of the most absurd-sounding labels used by Islamists to denote their enemies is probably 'Crusader-Zionists'. But as Mona Hammad and Edward Peters have recently shown, this label is indeed echoing a self-description of some Jewish settlers in the 1940s who connected the Zionist movement with the legacy of the Crusader states, and this did not go unnoticed in the Arabic-Muslim press of their neighbours.[38] Therefore, fitting this argument of the importance of the mediating role of nineteenth- and early twentieth-century medievalisms, a label like 'Crusader-Zionists' probably does not refer to the medieval crusades, but it obviously pertains to revived and recreated pasts of the mid-twentieth century. The structural amnesia of historicism again obstructs our understanding of how such pasts might gain relevance again and resurface in unexpected coherences.

Another characteristic example for the consequences of this structural amnesia in historicism are popular myths of the crusades.[39] In the introduction to the latest and most comprehensive work by Alfred Andrea and Andrew Holt, they state that crusade historians today:

> are united in the battle to correct the oversimplifications, misstatements, errors, and downright bizarre theories and beliefs that pervade *popular* perceptions and depictions of the crusades. For lack of a better term, crusade historians refer to these inaccuracies as "crusade myths".[40]

Actually, almost any study on crusader medievalism might in this sense be understood as dealing with crusade myths. But the authors of these books and articles insist on debunking *popular*, that is, *non-academic*, uses and abuses of 'real' crusade history, therefore carefully erecting a wall between the allegedly 'correct' academic knowledge and 'wrong' appropriations of this body of knowledge.

Yet this seems a contradiction in terms because most of these myths were not brought into existence by obscure conspiracy theorists; instead, most of them derive their origin from the very heart of crusade historiography. A few historiographical studies have already shown how much sedimented layers of interpretation still influence academic *and* popular representations of the crusades today.[41] But more important may be to note that many of the so-called crusade myths are 'rehashed' and residual older interpretations from crusade historiography that have made their ways into school books and 'popular scientific' (*populärwissenschaftlich*) representations of the crusades because they once represented the state of the art. A non-academic audience might still believe in the plausibility and truthfulness of these representations, while the academic community of crusade historians might already have left them behind for good. The persistence of the now disqualified crusade myths is obviously also a question of temporality – it takes a while until new academic insights and findings are disseminated into school books, for example. At the same time, we should not forget that what some crusade historians may debunk as myths are often still upheld as appropriate understandings of the crusades by other colleagues.[42]

While it is important to address crusade myths and disseminate new understandings of the crusading past into the public sphere, it is not very helpful to simply point out the lack of historical accuracy of such myths. Instead, it seems to be necessary to also explain *how* and *why* historians arrive at certain conclusions and interpretations, and how they are sometimes able to disprove certain images of the crusading past. This reveals to a non-academic audience the complexity not only of a historical phenomenon like the crusades itself but also how the discursive nature of historical research, the situatedness of our knowledge and the continual process of revisionism shapes the different layers of recreated pasts.

This approach also needs to engage with two problematic historiographical strategies that are found with most discussions of alleged crusade myths and other forms of crusader medievalisms. The first strategy is to call into question the expertise and academic reputation of those scholars who express opinions and interpretations mainstream historians do not – or not any longer – share. When certain authors and journalists voice visions of the crusades that some influential, professional crusade historians judge as inappropriate, their criticism can be extremely harsh, as for example levelled against people like Terry Jones[43] and Amin Maalouf,[44] whose documentary and books respectively are still extremely popular and translated into many languages. The same is true for intellectuals who were not trained as crusade historians but may well be understood as scholars like Karen Armstrong,[45] for example, or, from the other side of the political spectrum, Rodney Stark and Robert Spencer.[46] This strategy might even affect once highly esteemed crusade historians. For example, Joseph François Michaud[47] was recently called 'a royalist and journalist, and by no means a serious scholar' and Sir Steven Runciman's *A History of the Crusades*[48] was called 'a morality play pretending to be serious history'.[49]

Criticism of *the content* of the writings of these scholars seems appropriate to me, as most of them are highly problematic both in their ideology-based interpretations and in their naïve dealings with historical sources. Nevertheless, to simply deny their expertise and reputation seems unhelpful, especially as they are so extremely popular with non-academic audiences. More preferable would be a thorough historicisation and contextualisation of their works, also to disclose their technical deficiencies in reviving and recreating the crusading past. An ethically responsible way to engage with their crusader medievalisms might also be to acknowledge that they are, at least to some extent, mirroring and echoing the internal diversity of Crusade Studies past and present.

But the main problem, and probably an explanation for their success with non-academic audiences, at least with the works of Jones, Maalouf, Armstrong, Stark and Spencer, is that they are selling oversimplified master narratives of heroes and villains. For the first three the villains are the 'crusader barbarians,' and for the other two scholars the villains are the 'Muslim barbarians'. The 'success' of the latter three might also be explained by the way they are presenting the present state of the world – as in genealogical continuity with the medieval past.[50]

And this observation leads to the second problematic strategy in debunking crusade myths – that is to counter oversimplifications with other ahistorical explanatory models. This strategy becomes most visible where crusade historians are trying to refute the myth that the crusades were unprovoked acts of military aggression against the Muslim world.

Crusade historiography in the 'Clash of Civilizations' trap

The idea that the medieval crusades might be a helpful historical reference point to explain and understand the roots of the religiously legitimated violence of our own age has very much to do with the success of the 'Clash of Civilizations' concept outside *and* inside academia. The emergence of the 'Clash' concept, especially in that version which focuses on the troubled relationship between 'Islam and the West' (a highly problematic concept itself),[51] may be read as a symptom, a diagnosis and as a self-fulfilling prophecy at the same time. Samuel Huntington – who made this concept (in)famous – had originally designed it as a model to predict the future of 'International Relations' (IR) after the end of the so-called Cold War World Order'.[52] It was Bernard Lewis who not only invented the term, but also used it to explain the relationship of 'Islam and the West' in both past and present. Whatever one might personally think of the reliability and expertise of Lewis,[53] for this present argument it is important to note that he introduced the concept of the 'Clash of Civilizations' to the field of Medieval Studies as a way to understand the historical roots of present atrocities committed in the name of Allah.[54]

In the direct aftermath of 9/11 one of the arguments to be found in the public sphere was that because of the crusades the battle between Islam and the West, the 'Clash of Civilizations' began.[55] This argument is closely related to an abridged version of the critique of Orientalism,[56] condemning the alleged everlasting urge of 'the West' to dominate and subjugate 'the Orient' as well as condemning the supposed inherently violent character of Christian Western societies.[57] There were even voices to be found after the events of 9/11, most prominently Karen Armstrong, who characterised these attacks as an overdue – and if not justified, but at least to a certain extent reasonable – response to the long historical tradition of Western atrocities against Muslim societies.[58] That crusade historians felt the urge to refute the 'myth' that recent Islamist violence was a direct reaction to the crusades (with a delay of 900 years) is understandable. But the idea that the crusades, and especially the brutal conquest of Jerusalem in 1099, might have caused a severe trauma in the Muslim world is still hotly debated.[59]

While it would have been a sound and legitimate task to contextualise and historicise, and thereby to refute, the myth of the crusades being the reason for the 9/11 attacks, some intellectuals used the concept of the 'Clash of Civilizations' to simply turn the argument around, portraying religious violence as deeply rooted in Islamic culture and religion itself. In this version, the crusades were presented as an early, necessary attempt to stop the violent sprawl of Islam. Ironically, both camps utilise the 'Clash of Civilizations' paradigm (more or less consciously) to very different ends and meanings – the only methodological difference lies in the determination of the starting point, or rather in the enshrinement of different fetishized origins.[60] This simply enshrines even older roots (622 AD instead of 1099, so to say) and redistributes the roles of heroes and villains in the blame game.

Some crusade historians do not confine themselves to explain the immediate historical, political and military backgrounds for the crusades in the eleventh century when trying to confront this myth. In one of his popular articles on crusade myths Thomas Madden wrote the following:

> From the time of Mohammed, Muslims had sought to conquer the Christian world. They did a pretty good job of it, too. [...] As far as unprovoked aggression goes, it was all on the Muslim side. At some point what was left of the Christian world would have to defend itself or simply succumb to Islamic conquest. [...] In other words, the Crusades were from the beginning a defensive war. The entire history of the eastern Crusades is one of response to Muslim aggression.[61]

Paul Crawford's contribution to the *Seven Myths of the Crusades* sticks very closely to this explanatory model but goes further by adopting a historiographical narrative to be found in most of the medieval crusade propaganda.[62] He begins with a short anti-hagiographical account of the rise of Islam; then enlists places, regions and whole countries which used to belong to Christianity, elaborating how they were venerated by Christians, to conclude how each and every single one of them were lost to Islam due to its everlasting *jihad*. This narrative seems problematic to me on different levels. Primarily, while Crawford is battling against alleged distortions of crusade history by non-professional crusade scholars, he presents early Islamic history and early medieval Christian-Muslim relations in almost the same 'mythical' manner, seeming to ignore the many recent interpretations that counter his representation.[63] Secondly, he might be too enthusiastic in embracing the ideological self-legitimisation of medieval crusaders. Thirdly, the chapter takes for granted the logic of the 'Clash' – that of a perpetual violent encounter between incompatible civilizational units – which foregrounds Christian-Muslim violent encounters and has little room for peaceful encounters or Christian-Christian violence. The First Crusade was defensive because of its temporal location in this schema; the origin point was the emergence of Islam and the subsequent Islamic invasions of the seventh century:

> The crusades were merely another aspect of the conflict that had existed between Islam and Christianity (and Islam and Judaism) since Islam's inception. As the First Crusade began, a new chapter was indeed being written... but in a book that was already very old.[64]

It almost seems ironic that Madden and Crawford (and others) do not actually deconstruct the myth of the crusades being a 'Clash of Civilizations' between 'Islam and the West' that led to the terrorist attacks in the twenty-first century. Instead, this impression is sustained by not only prolonging the history of this 'titanic struggle' but even by de-historicising it. To be more precise, a double movement of disconnecting and connecting is at work here. While the crusades are securely stored in the medieval dead past, as disconnected from Western modernity, Islamist violence is 'fetishized' as the essence of Islam, reifying the image of the everlasting medieval-ness of Muslims. Although none of these scholars go so far as to name the recent Islamist terrorist attacks as the natural consequence of Islam's alleged everlasting *jihad*, this may seem – at least to some readers – as the next logical step.[65]

Of perhaps greatest concern is that those who commit violence in the name of Allah, those who want to fight the terrorists, those who

are afraid of an 'Islamization' of the West and especially many of those
who try to make sense of the recent massive resurgence of religiously
legitimated violence – so many of them implicitly or explicitly frame
these phenomena as symptoms of the everlasting 'Clash of Civilizations' between 'Islam and the West.' Facing the early success of this
'identity trap' of culturalising (and de-historicising) recent conflicts
and problems, Noble Prize Winner Amartya Sen in his essay on 'Identity and Violence' from 2006 wrote the following:

> Modern conflicts, which cannot be adequately analyzed without
> going into contemporary events and machinations, are then in-
> terpreted as ancient feuds which allegedly place today's players
> in preordained roles in an allegedly ancestral play. [...] It invokes
> the richness of history and the apparent depth and gravity of cul-
> tural analysis, and it seeks profundity in a way that an immedi-
> ate political analysis of the 'here and now'—seen as ordinary and
> mundane—would seem to lack.[66]

If even academics with authoritative voices claim that Christian-
Muslim relations in the Middle Ages are the point of origin, the *roots*
of contemporary conflicts and acts of violence, they bestow these recent phenomena with an almost mystical depth and meaningfulness.
Historical narratives based on the logic of the 'Clash' are buying into
a Manichean world view presenting the recreated pasts as a version of
'providential history' (*Heilsgeschichte*).

The fuzziness of history

While the revived and recreated crusading pasts are indeed a worthy
object of historical study, I have tried to identify issues that require a
particular hermeneutical and methodological sensitivity. It is not necessary for current Crusade Studies to 'overidentify' with the research
object, that is to sympathetically adopt arguments in defence of the
crusades from the medieval source material. Nor is it helpful to simply
counter revived crusading pasts in political and violent contexts with
images of a peaceful coexistence of Muslims, Christians and Jews as
the 'real' history of the Middle Ages, by writing out the unpleasant
parts. To answer oversimplifications with other oversimplifications
does not seem to be an effective way to engage with the emotive power
of revived and recreated pasts. Forcing the manifold layers of academically recreated pasts into monolithic, monocausal master narratives

is one of the major factors that enables certain people and groups to hijack parts of history for their own purposes. As Nicholas Morton recently put it in regard to the First Crusade:

> Recognising the messiness and convoluted nature of the First Crusade is important. Too often history is reduced to a simple matter of political slogans. It is far easier to remember and shout the mantra 'the Crusade was a Christian versus Muslim war' than it is to reconstruct the full complexity of these events. Recognising that complexity is essential in a day and age when there are many slogans yet little understanding.[67]

What is needed, I would suggest, is a *relentless* historicisation and contextualisation of *all* the interpretations, images and master narratives about the historical crusades *and* their relevance for today. This goes for any kind of crusader medievalism – spanning academic historiography, popular science and all the other more or less creative appropriations of crusade history. It might also be a helpful way to finally overcome the structural amnesia in common historiographical practice.

To explain the difficulties of reconstructing history may also assist people outside of academia to understand why there exist so many conflicting interpretations of a phenomenon like the crusades. As our reconstructions are always just *attempts*, the work always remains unfinished, and later generations will almost certainly come to other conclusions than earlier ones. Even within a limited timeframe, different scholars advocate different positions. That of course does not only stem from the openness and ambivalences of the source material but also from the different disciplinary perspectives with which crusade scholars work. But more importantly, it relates to every scholar's self-perception and his or her attitudes towards the present times. John Tolan in his book *Saint Francis and the Sultan* put it provocatively:

> I can only observe that modesty behoves the historian who, in gazing into the murky waters of the past, may see above all his own reflection, the image of his hopes and fears.[68]

If it is not for the historian to voice this unpopular admission, who else should do it?

Notes

1 See Gadi Algazi, 'Forget Memory: Some Critical Remarks on Memory, Forgetting and History', in *Damnatio in Memoria: Deformation und*

Gegenkonstruktionen in der Geschichte, eds. Sebastian Scholz, Gerald Schwedler and Kai-Michael Sprenger (Köln, 2014), p. 8ff. He objects that this kind of structural amnesia is only a limited kind of forgetting, not a literal amnesia.

2 Benjamin Z. Kedar, 'Crusade Historians and the Massacres of 1096', *Jewish History* 12 (1998), p. 11.

3 See Jörn Rüsen, *Evidence and Meaning: A Theory of Historical Studies*, eds. Diane Kerns and Katie Digan (New York, 2017); Chris Lorenz and Berber Bevernage, eds., *Breaking up Time: Negotiating the Borders Between Present, Past and Future* (Göttingen, 2013); Reinhart Koselleck, *The Practice of Conceptual History: Timing History, Spacing Concepts* (Stanford, CA, 2011).

4 For historicisation, see of Glenn W. Most, 'Historicization Reconsidered', in *Historisierung. Begriff – Methode – Praxis*, eds. Moritz Baumstark and Robert Forkel (Stuttgart, 2016), p. 37. See also the longer quotation below.

5 For reflections on the history of 'objectivity' see Lorraine Daston, 'Objectivity and the Escape from Perspective', *Social Studies of Science* 22 (1992), pp. 597–618.

6 Richard Utz, 'Coming to Terms with Medievalism', *European Journal of English Studies* 15 (2011), p. 102.

7 Achim Landwehr, *Die anwesende Abwesenheit der Vergangenheit. Essay zur Geschichtstheorie* (Frankfurt am Main, 2016), especially the chapters on 'Chronoferenz' and 'Zeitschaft', pp. 149–65, 281–316.

8 Most, 'Historicization Reconsidered', p. 37.

9 Fernando Coronil, 'Beyond Occidentalism: Toward Nonimperial Geohistorical Categories', *Cultural Anthropology* 11 (1996), pp. 51–87.

10 See Paul Chevedden's thorough critique of Pope Urban II's call for a crusade at the Council of Clermont in 1095 as 'the big bang theory' in Crusade Studies: Paul E. Chevedden, 'Crusade Creationism versus Pope Urban II's Conceptualization of the Crusades', *The Historian* 75 (2013), pp. 1–46.

11 Marc Bloch, *The Historian's Craft* (Manchester, 2004), pp. 24–28.

12 Gabrielle M. Spiegel, 'Revising the Past/Revisiting the Present. How Change Happens in Historiography', *History and Theory* 46 (2007), pp. 1–19.

13 Richard J. Utz, *Medievalism: A Manifesto* (Kalamazoo, 2017), p. 81.

14 Kathleen Biddick interpreted the artificial separation of medievalism and Medieval Studies during the nineteenth century as a trauma that still haunts medievalists (most obviously in the Anglophone context) today; Kathleen Biddick, *The Shock of Medievalism* (Durham, NC, 1998).

15 Utz, *Medievalism*. Although he does not use these labels.

16 Mike Horswell, *The Rise and Fall of British Crusader Medievalism, c.1825–1945* (London, 2018).

17 Jonathan Riley-Smith, *The Crusades, Christianity, and Islam* (New York, 2008); Siberry, *New Crusaders*; Knobler, 'Holy Wars'.

18 Kerwin L. Klein, 'On the Emergence of Memory in Historical Discourse', *Representations* 69 (2000), p. 128.

19 Wulf Kansteiner, 'Finding Meaning in Memory: A Methodological Critique of Collective Memory Studies', *History and Theory* 41 (2002), p. 180.

20 Andrea and Holt below.

21 Gabrielle M. Spiegel, 'The Future of the Past', *Journal of the Philosophy of History* 8 (2014), p. 168.

126   *Kristin Skottki*

22 This is also one of the main arguments of Brian Johnsrud, 'Metaphorical Memories of the Medieval Crusades after 9/11', in *Memory Unbound: Tracing the Dynamics of Memory Studies*, eds. Lucy Bond, Stef Craps and Pieter Vermeulen (New York, 2017), pp. 195–218. Although I think he underestimates the role of academic historians in the public sphere.
23 Utz, *Medievalism*, p. 85ff.: 'In fact, medievalism and medieval studies have a mutually beneficial relationship, and a thorough understanding of the broader cultural phenomenon of medievalism enhances academic medievalists' tool kits by increasing their theoretical sophistication, critical self-awareness, and social impact.'
24 Jonathan Riley-Smith, *The First Crusade and the Idea of Crusading* (London, 2003); Jonathan Riley-Smith, *The Crusades: A History* (London, 2009).
25 Norman Housley, *Contesting the Crusades* (Malden, MA, 2006), pp. 1–23.
26 Akil N. Awan, Andrew Hoskins and Ben O'Loughlin, eds., *Radicalisation and Media: Connectivity and Terrorism in the New Media Ecology* (London, 2012).
27 Andrew B. R. Elliott, *Medievalism, Politics and Mass Media: Appropriating the Middle Ages in the Twenty-First Century* (Woodbridge, 2017). But see my critical comments below.
28 Brian Johnsrud, 'The Da Vinci Code, Crusade Conspiracies, and the Clash of Historiographies', in *Conspiracy Theories in the United States and the Middle East: A Comparative Approach*, eds. Michael Butter and Maurus Reinkowski (Berlin, 2014), pp. 100–117.
29 See the personal account of this change by Thomas F. Madden, 'Inventing the Crusades', *First Things* (June 2009), <www.firstthings.com/article/2009/06/inventing-the-crusades>, [accessed 9 January 2018].
30 E.g. Charlotte Edwardes, 'Ridley Scott's New Crusades Film "Panders to Osama bin Laden"', *The Telegraph* 18 January 2004, <http://www.telegraph.co.uk/news/worldnews/northamerica/usa/1452000/Ridley-Scotts-new-Crusades-film-panders-to-Osama-bin-Laden.html>, [accessed 9 January 2018].
31 E.g. Paul Sturtevant, 'Kingdom of Heaven's Road Map for Peace', *Bulletin of International Medieval Research* 12 (2006), pp. 23–39.
32 Johnsrud, 'Metaphorical Memories'.
33 Jonathan Hsy, 'The Middle Ages, the Crusades, and the Alt-Right: A Symposium', (13 October 2017), <https://storify.com/JonathanHsy/the-middle-ages-the-crusades-and-the-alt-right-a-s>, [accessed 6 December 2017].
34 Elliott, *Medievalism*.
35 Ibid., p. 17.
36 Ibid., p. 37.
37 Bruce Holsinger, *Neomedievalism, Neoconservatism, and the War on Terror* (Chicago, 2007).
38 Mona Hammad and Edward Peters, 'Islam and the Crusades. A Nine-Hundred-Year-Long Grievance?', in, *Seven Myths of the Crusades*, eds. Alfred Andrea and Andrew Holt. Myths of History (Indianapolis, IN and Cambridge, MA, 2015), p. 145ff., with references to the already existing, mostly Israeli, studies of this phenomenon.

39 See the bibliographical references in Andrea and Holt, 'Introduction', *Seven Myths*, p. xxxff. with notes 72–77. Cf. also Nikolas Jaspert, 'Ein Polymythos: Die Kreuzzüge', in *Mythen in der Geschichte*, eds. Helmut Altrichter, Klaus Herbers and Helmut Neuhaus (Freiburg i. Br., 2004), pp. 203–35.

40 Andrea and Holt, 'Introduction', *Seven Myths*, p. xix. My emphasis.

41 Benjamin Z. Kedar, 'The Jerusalem Massacre of July 1099 in the Western Historiography of the Crusades', *Crusades* 3 (2004), pp. 15–75; Christopher Tyerman, *The Debate on the Crusades* (Manchester, 2012).

42 See for example the myth that younger sons from noble families were sent on crusades to find themselves an inheritance in the East, debunked by Jessalynn Bird, 'The Crusades: Eschatological Lemmings, Younger Sons, Papal Hegemony, and Colonialism', in *Misconceptions about the Middle Ages*, eds. Stephen J. Harris and Bryon L. Grigsby (New York, 2008), p. 85. But still upheld as an explanation, for example, by Peter Thorau, *Die Kreuzzüge* (München, 2004), p. 39.

43 His (in)famous documentary series is thoroughly discussed in Andrea and Holt, 'Introduction', *Seven Myths*, pp. xxiv–xxvi. Cf. also the book version Terry Jones and Alan Ereira, *Crusades* (New York, 1995).

44 Amin Maalouf, *The Crusades Through Arab Eyes* (London, 1984). But see positive evaluation of his work by Hamid Bahri and Francesca Canadé Sautman, 'Crossing History, Dis-Orienting the Orient: Amin Maalouf's Uses of the Medieval', in *Medievalisms in the Postcolonial World: The Idea of 'the Middle Ages' Outside Europe*, eds. Kathleen Davis and Nadia Altschul (Baltimore, 2009), pp. 174–205.

45 Karen Armstrong, *Holy War: The Crusades and Their Impact on Today's World* (New York, 2001). See the documentation of the criticism by Andrew P. Holt, 'Crusade Historians and Karen Armstrong', (1 June 2016). <https://apholt.com/2016/06/01/crusade-historians-and-karen-armstrong/>, [accessed 6 December 2017].

46 Rodney Stark, *God's Battalions: The Case for the Crusades* (New York, 2009); Robert Spencer, *The Politically Incorrect Guide to Islam (and the Crusades)* (Washington, DC, 2005). For a trenchant discussion of these two works see Johnsrud, 'Metaphorical Memories', pp. 208–13.

47 Joseph François Michaud, *Histoire des croisades,* 7 vols. (Paris, 1811–1822). See also the critical assessment of his work by Kim Munholland, 'Michaud's History of the Crusades and the French Crusade in Algeria under Louis-Philippe', in *The Popularization of Images: Visual Culture Under the July Monarchy*, eds. Petra ten-Doesschate Chu and Gabriel P. Weisberg (Princeton, NJ, 1994), pp. 144–65.

48 Steven Runciman, *A History of the Crusades,* 3 vols. (Cambridge, 1951–1954).

49 Andrea and Holt, 'Introduction', *Seven Myths*, pp. xxi and xxiii.

50 For a thorough critique of this genealogical thinking in Crusade Studies see Geraldine G. Heng, 'Holy War Redux: The Crusades, Futures of the Past, and Strategic Logic in the 'Clash' of Religions', *Publications of the Modern Language Association of America* 126 (2011), pp. 422–31.

51 Not only does this concept play off a religion against a geographical entity, it is also based on a vision of monolithic, mutually exclusive

civilisations, denying the entangled nature of geography and history. See, again, Coronil, 'Beyond Occidentalism', p. 77ff.

52 Samuel Huntington, 'The Clash of Civilizations?', *Foreign Affairs* 71 (1993), pp. 22–49; with later book versions; *contra*, (amongst others), Kurt Villads Jensen, 'Cultural Encounters and Clash of Civilisations: Huntington and Modern Crusade Studies', *Cultural Encounters during the Crusades*, eds. Kurt Villads Jensen, Kirsi Salonen and Helle Vogt (Odense, 2013), pp. 15–26.

53 For example, see the critique by John Trumpbour, 'The Clash of Civilizations. Samuel P. Huntington, Bernard Lewis, and the Remaking of the Post-Cold War World Order', in *The New Crusades: Constructing the Muslim Enemy*, eds. Emran Qureshi and Michael A. Sells (New York, 2003), pp. 88–130; Holsinger, *Neomedievalism*.

54 Bernard Lewis, 'The Roots of Muslim Rage', *The Atlantic Monthly* (3 September 1990). <www.theatlantic.com/magazine/archive/1990/09/the-roots-of-muslim-rage/304643/>, [accessed 9 December 2017].

55 Tariq Ali, *The Clash of Fundamentalisms: Crusades, Jihads and Modernity* (London, 2002).

56 Orientalism was most prominently criticized by Edward W. Said in his *Orientalism* (New York, 2003), p. 3.

57 See the discussion of the negative attitudes towards the crusades dominating the public sphere for most of the second half of the twentieth century in Jaspert, 'Ein Polymythos'.

58 She wrote: 'It is now over a millennium since Pope Urban II called the First Crusade in 1095, but the hatred and suspicion that this expedition unleashed still reverberates, never more so than on September 11, 2001, and during the terrible days that followed.', Armstrong, *Holy War*, p. ix (Preface to the second edition).

59 Affirmative: Karen Armstrong, 'The Crusades, Even Now', *The New York Times Magazine* (19 November 1999), <www.nytimes.com/library/magazine/millennium/m4/armstrong.html>, [accessed 4 October 2012]; but see the thorough, critical analysis in Hammad and Peters, 'Islam and the Crusades', *Seven Myths*.

60 Again, see Heng, 'Holy War Redux'.

61 Thomas F. Madden, 'Crusade Myths', *Catholic Dossier* (1, 2002), <www.ignatius insight.com/features2005/tmadden_crusademyths_feb05.asp>, [accessed 9 January 2018]. See also Thomas F. Madden, *The Crusades Controversy: Setting the Record Straight* (North Palm Beach, FL, 2017).

62 Paul Crawford, 'The First Crusade: Unprovoked Offense or Overdue Defense?', in Andrea and Holt, *Seven Myths*, pp. 1–28.

63 Fred M. Donner, *Muhammad and the Believers. At the Origins of Islam* (Cambridge, MA, 2010).

64 Crawford, 'First Crusade', p. 28.

65 Elliott, *Medievalism,* p. 153: 'Breivik makes no distinction between his quotations from books on the crusades by Thomas Madden, a recognised historian and expert on Islam and the crusades, and 'books' such as the *Politically Incorrect Guide to Islam (and the Crusades)* by Robert Spencer, a blogger for the extremist website JihadWatch.' While Elliott uses this example to demonstrate how non-referential terrorist Breivik's vision of the crusading past was, one may also wonder if, for Breivik, the messages

of Spencer and Madden were not, at least to a certain extent, aiming in the same direction.

66 Amartya Sen, *Identity and Violence: The Illusion of Destiny* (New York, 2006), p. 43.
67 Nicholas Morton, 'Was the First Crusade Really a War Against Islam?', *History Today* 67 (2017) <www.historytoday.com/nicholas-morton/was-first-crusade-really-war-against-islam>, [accessed 13 November 2017].
68 John Victor Tolan, *Saint Francis and the Sultan. The Curious History of a Christian- Muslim Encounter* (Oxford, 2009), p. 327.

References

Algazi, Gadi. 'Forget Memory: Some Critical Remarks on Memory, Forgetting and History'. In *Damnatio in memoria: Deformation und Gegenkonstruktionen in der Geschichte.* eds. Sebastian Scholz, Gerald Schwedler and Kai-Michael Sprenger. Köln: Böhlau, 2014. pp. 25–34.

Ali, Tariq. *The Clash of Fundamentalisms: Crusades, Jihads and Modernity.* London: Verso, 2002.

Andrea, Alfred J., and Andrew P. Holt. 'Introduction. Once More into the Breach: The Continuing War against Crusade Myths'. In Seven Myths of the Crusades. eds. Andrea and Holt, pp. xi–xxxvi.

———, eds. *Seven Myths of the Crusades. Myths of History.* Indianapolis, IN & Cambridge, MA: Hackett, 2015.

Armstrong, Karen. 'The Crusades, Even Now'. *The New York Times Magazine,* November 19, 1999. www.nytimes.com/library/magazine/millennium/m4/armstrong.html. [Accessed 4 October 2012].

———. *Holy War: The Crusades and Their Impact on Today's World.* 2nd edn. New York: Anchor Books, 2001.

Awan, Akil N., Andrew Hoskins, and Ben O'Loughlin, eds. *Radicalisation and Media: Connectivity and Terrorism in the New Media Ecology.* London: Routledge, 2012.

Bahri, Hamid, and Francesca Canadé Sautman. 'Crossing History, Dis-Orienting the Orient: Amin Maalouf's Uses of the Medieval'. In *Medievalisms in the Postcolonial World: The Idea of 'the Middle Ages' Outside Europe.* eds. Kathleen Davis and Nadia Altschul. Baltimore: Johns Hopkins University Press, 2009. pp. 174–205.

Biddick, Kathleen. *The Shock of Medievalism.* Durham, NC: Duke University Press, 1998.

Bird, Jessalynn. 'The Crusades: Eschatological Lemmings, Younger Sons, Papal Hegemony, and Colonialism'. In *Misconceptions about the Middle Ages.* eds. Stephen J. Harris and Bryon L. Grigsby. New York: Routledge, 2008. pp. 85–89.

Bloch, Marc. *The Historian's Craft.* Manchester: MUP, 2004.

Chevedden, Paul E. 'Crusade Creationism versus Pope Urban II's Conceptualization of the Crusades'. *The Historian* 75 (2013), pp. 1–46.

Coronil, Fernando. 'Beyond Occidentalism: Toward Nonimperial Geohistorical Categories'. *Cultural Anthropology* 11 (1996), pp. 51–87.

Crawford, Paul. 'The First Crusade: Unprovoked Offense or Overdue Defense'? In *Seven Myths of the Crusades*. ed. Andrea and Holt. Indianapolis, IN: Hackett Publishing Company, Inc., 2015 pp. 1–28.

Daston, Lorraine. 'Objectivity and the Escape from Perspective'. *Social Studies of Science* 22 (1992), pp. 597–618.

Donner, Fred M. *Muhammad and the Believers. At the Origins of Islam*. Cambridge, MA: The Belknap Press of Harvard University Press, 2010.

Edwardes, Charlotte. 'Ridley Scott's New Crusades Film 'Panders to Osama bin Laden''. *The Telegraph* (18 January 2004), www.telegraph.co.uk/news/worldnews/northamerica/usa/1452000/Ridley-Scotts-new-Crusades-film-panders-to-Osama-bin-Laden.html. [Accessed 9 December 2017].

Elliott, Andrew B. R. *Medievalism, Politics and Mass Media: Appropriating the Middle Ages in the Twenty-First Century*. Woodbridge: Boydell & Brewer, 2017.

Hammad, Mona, and Edward Peters. 'Islam and the Crusades. A Nine-Hundred-Year-Long Grievance?' In *Seven Myths of the Crusades*. eds. Andrea and Holt. Indianapolis, IN: Hackett Publishing Company, Inc., 2015 pp. 127–49.

Heng, Geraldine G. 'Holy War Redux: The Crusades, Futures of the Past, and Strategic Logic in the 'Clash' of Religions'. *Publications of the Modern Language Association of America* 126 (2011), pp. 422–31.

Holsinger, Bruce. *Neomedievalism, Neoconservatism, and the War on Terror*. Chicago, IL: Prickly Paradigm Press, 2007.

Holt, Andrew P. 'Crusade Historians and Karen Armstrong'. In Andrew Holt, Ph.D. - History, Religion, and Foreign Affairs (personal blog) (1 June 2016). https://apholt.com/2016/06/01/crusade-historians-and-karen-armstrong/. [Accessed 6 December 2017].

Horswell, Mike. *The Rise and Fall of British Crusader Medievalism, c.1825–1945*. London: Routledge, 2018.

Housley, Norman. *Contesting the Crusades*. Malden, MA: Blackwell, 2006.

Hsy, Jonathan. 'The Middle Ages, the Crusades, and the Alt-Right: A Symposium'. *Twitterfeed* #AltCrusade17 (13 October 2017). https://storify.com/JonathanHsy/the-middle-ages-the-crusades-and-the-alt-right-a-s. [Accessed 6 December 2017].

Huntington, Samuel. 'The Clash of Civilizations?' *Foreign Affairs* 71 (1993), pp. 22–49.

Jaspert, Nikolas. 'Ein Polymythos: Die Kreuzzüge.' In *Mythen in der Geschichte*. eds. Helmut Altrichter, Klaus Herbers, and Helmut Neuhaus. Freiburg i. Br.: Rombach, 2004. pp. 203–35.

Jensen, Kurt Villads. 'Cultural Encounters and Clash of Civilisations: Huntingdon and Modern Crusade Studies'. In *Cultural Encounters during the Crusades*. eds. Kurt Villads Jensen, Kirsi Salonen, and Helle Vogt. Odense: University of Southern Denmark Press, 2013. pp. 15–26.

Johnsrud, Brian. 'The Da Vinci Code, Crusade Conspiracies, and the Clash of Historiographies.' In *Conspiracy Theories in the United States and the*

Middle East: A Comparative Approach. eds. Michael Butter, and Maurus Reinkowski. Berlin: De Gruyter, 2014. pp. 100–17.

———. 'Metaphorical Memories of the Medieval Crusades after 9/11'. In *Memory Unbound: Tracing the Dynamics of Memory Studies.* eds. Lucy Bond, Stef Craps, and Pieter Vermeulen. New York: Berghahn Books, 2017. pp. 195–218.

Jones, Terry and Alan Ereira. *Crusades.* New York: Facts on File, 1995.

Kansteiner, Wulf. 'Finding Meaning in Memory: A Methodological Critique of Collective Memory Studies'. *History and Theory* 41 (2002), pp. 179–97.

Kedar, Benjamin Z. 'Crusade Historians and the Massacres of 1096'. *Jewish History* 12 (1998), pp. 11–31.

———. 'The Jerusalem Massacre of July 1099 in the Western Historiography of the Crusades'. *Crusades* 3 (2004), pp. 15–75.

Klein, Kerwin Lee. 'On the Emergence of Memory in Historical Discourse'. *Representations* 69 (2000), pp. 127–50.

Knobler, Adam. 'Holy Wars, Empires, and the Portability of the Past: The Modern Uses of Medieval Crusades'. *Comparative Studies in Society and History* 48 (2006), pp. 293–325.

Koselleck, Reinhart. *The Practice of Conceptual History: Timing History, Spacing Concepts.* Stanford, CA: Stanford University Press, 2011.

Landwehr, Achim. *Die anwesende Abwesenheit der Vergangenheit. Essay zur Geschichtstheorie.* Frankfurt am Main: Fischer, 2016.

Lewis, Bernard. 'The Roots of Muslim Rage'. *The Atlantic Monthly* 3 (September 1990). www.theatlantic.com/magazine/archive/1990/09/the-roots-of-muslim-rage/304643/. [Accessed 9 December 2017].

Lorenz, Chris and Berber Bevernage, eds. *Breaking Up Time: Negotiating the Borders Between Present, Past and Future.* Göttingen: Vandenhoeck & Ruprecht, 2013.

Maalouf, Amin. *The Crusades through Arab Eyes.* London: Al Saqi Books, 1984.

Madden, Thomas F. 'Crusade Myths'. *Catholic Dossier* 1 (2002). www.ignatius insight.com/features2005/tmadden_crusademyths_feb05.asp. [Accessed 9 January 2018].

———. 'Inventing the Crusades.' *First Things. Journal of the Institute on Religion and Public Life* (1 June 2009). www.firstthings.com/article/2009/06/inventing-the-crusades. [Accessed 9 January 2018].

———. *The Crusades Controversy: Setting the Record Straight.* North Palm Beach, FL: Beacon, 2017.

Michaud, Joseph François. *Histoire des croisades.* 7 Vols. Paris: Pillet, 1811–1822.

Morton, Nicholas. 'Was the First Crusade Really a War Against Islam?' *History Today* 67 (2017) www.historytoday.com/nicholas-morton/was-first-crusade-really-war-against-islam. [Accessed 13 November 2017].

Most, Glenn W. 'Historicization Reconsidered'. In *Historisierung. Begriff – Methode – Praxis.* eds. Moritz Baumstark and Robert Forkel. Stuttgart: Metzler Verlag, 2016. pp. 36–41.

132   *Kristin Skottki*

Munholland, Kim. 'Michaud's History of the Crusades and the French Crusade in Algeria under Louis-Philippe'. In *The Popularization of Images. Visual Culture under the July Monarchy.* eds. Petra ten-Doesschate Chu and Gabriel P. Weisberg. Princeton, NJ: Princeton University Press, 1994. pp. 144–65.

Riley-Smith, Jonathan. *The First Crusade and the Idea of Crusading.* London & New York: Continuum, 2003.

———. *The Crusades, Christianity, and Islam. The Bampton Lectures in America.* New York: Columbia University Press, 2008.

———. *The Crusades: A History.* 3rd edn. London: Continuum, 2009.

Runciman, Steven. *A History of the Crusades.* 3 Vols. Cambridge: Cambridge University Press, 1951–1954.

Rüsen, Jörn. *Evidence and Meaning: A Theory of Historical Studies.* New York: Berghahn, 2017.

Said, Edward W. *Orientalism. 25th Anniversary Edition with a New Preface by the Author.* New York: Vintage Books, 2003.

Sen, Amartya. *Identity and Violence: The Illusion of Destiny.* New York: Norton, 2006.

Siberry, Elizabeth. *The New Crusaders: Images of the Crusades in the Nineteenth and Early Twentieth Centuries.* Aldershot: Ashgate, 2000.

Spencer, Robert. *The Politically Incorrect Guide to Islam (and the Crusades).* Washington, DC: Regnery, 2005.

Spiegel, Gabrielle. 'Revising the Past/Revisiting the Present. How Change Happens in Historiography'. *History and Theory* 46 (2007), pp. 1–19.

———. 'The Future of the Past'. *Journal of the Philosophy of History* 8 (2014), pp. 149–79.

Stark, Rodney. *God's Battalions: The Case for the Crusades.* New York: Harper One, 2009.

Sturtevant, Paul. 'Kingdom of Heaven's Road Map for Peace'. *Bulletin of International Medieval Research* 12 (2006), pp. 23–39.

Thorau, Peter. *Die Kreuzzüge.* München: Beck, 2004.

Tolan, John Victor. *Saint Francis and the Sultan: The Curious History of a Christian-Muslim Encounter.* Oxford: OUP, 2009.

Trumpbour, John. 'The Clash of Civilizations. Samuel P. Huntington, Bernard Lewis, and the Remaking of the Post-Cold War World Order'. In *The New Crusades. Constructing the Muslim Enemy.* eds. Emran Qureshi and Michael A. Sells. New York: Columbia University Press. 2003, pp. 88–130.

Tyerman, Christopher. *The Debate on the Crusades.* Manchester: MUP, 2012.

Utz, Richard. 'Coming to Terms with Medievalism'. *European Journal of English Studies* 15 (2011), pp. 101–14.

———. *Medievalism: A Manifesto.* Kalamazoo, MI: ARC Humanities Press, 2017.

Index

For Product Safety Concerns and Information please contact our EU
representative GPSR@taylorandfrancis.com
Taylor & Francis Verlag GmbH, Kaufingerstraße 24, 80331 München, Germany

www.ingramcontent.com/pod-product-compliance
Ingram Content Group UK Ltd.
Pitfield, Milton Keynes, MK11 3LW, UK
UKHW021424080625
459435UK00011B/142